Food in Missouri

Project Sponsors

Missouri Humanities Council and the National Endowment
for the Humanities

Missouri State Library

Western Historical Manuscript Collection, University of
Missouri–Columbia

Project Directors

Susanna Alexander

Rebecca B. Schroeder

Consultants

Virginia Lee Fisher

Howard W. Marshall

Adolf E. Schroeder

Arvarh E. Strickland

Special Thanks

Luke Dudenhoeffer

Randy Ennis

Kathy Flippin

Philippe A. Habassi

Cynthia Hagenoff

Dealia Lipscomb

Mary Shopper

Dorothy Sutton

Adult Learning Center, Columbia

ABLE Learning Center, Jefferson City

Daniel Boone Regional Library, Columbia

Missouri Folklore Society

State Historical Society of Missouri

Missouri Heritage Readers

General Editor, Rebecca B. Schroeder

Each Missouri Heritage Reader explores a particular aspect of the state's rich cultural heritage. Focusing on people, places, historical events, and the details of daily life, these books illustrate the ways in which people from all parts of the world contributed to the development of the state and the region. The books incorporate documentary and oral history, folklore, and informal literature in a way that makes these resources accessible to all Missourians.

Intended primarily for adult new readers, these books will also be invaluable to readers of all ages interested in the cultural and social history of Missouri.

Books in the Series

Food in Missouri

A Cultural Stew

Madeline Matson

University of Missouri Press

COLUMBIA AND LONDON

Library of Congress Cataloging-in-Publication Data

Matson, Madeline.
    Food in Missouri : a cultural stew / Madeline Matson.
        p.   cm.—(Missouri heritage readers)
    Includes bibliographical references and index.
    ISBN 0-8262-0960-2 (pbk.)
    1. Food habits—Missouri—History. 2. Cookery—Missouri—
    History. I. Title. II. Series
    GT2853.U5M38   1994   93–50819
    394.1'2'09778—dc20   CIP

∞™ This paper meets the requirements of the
American National Standard for Permanence of Paper
for Printed Library Materials, Z39.48, 1984.

Designer: Elizabeth K. Fett
Typesetter: Connell-Zeko Type & Graphics
Printer and binder: Thomson-Shore, Inc.
Typefaces: Goudy Old Style and Omega

The publication of this book has been supported by a grant from

MISSOURI
HUMANITIES
COUNCIL

This book is dedicated to my family, who taught me the importance of community and food traditions and encouraged my interest in food. It is especially dedicated to my mother, who gave me some of the finest food memories anyone could hope for.

Contents

Acknowledgments

Thanks to my family and friends who provided support during the writing of this book; to my assistant, Patti Dudenhoeffer; to the reference staff of the Missouri State Library; to Bob Dyer and Margot Ford McMillen for their helpful suggestions; and to Becky Schroeder for her patience and invaluable editorial help.

Food in Missouri

A Taste of Missouri

We must eat to live and live to eat.

—Henry Fielding

Missouri's food history has been shaped by many forces— from the rivers, the soil, and the climate to the traditions of the people who settled this diverse land and made it productive. What Missourians eat today reflects the contributions of Native Americans, of the Africans who were brought to Missouri as early as the eighteenth century, and of the British and other European settlers who came to Missouri in the eighteenth and nineteenth centuries. This blending of cultures continues to the present day with immigrants from Asia and Latin America. All have enriched and added unique ingredients to our "cultural stew."

Native American Foods

About twenty thousand years ago, the ancestors of the people we call American Indians crossed a narrow strip of land and ice that connected Asia and North America. This strip is now covered with water. The people were hunters, and they traveled south into the Americas, eventually settling in all regions of the continents. Their travels took place over thousands of years.

The first "Missourians" arrived more than ten thousand years ago. They hunted large animals, using spears with stone points. Among the animals they hunted were giant ground sloths and mastodons—huge, hairy creatures that resembled elephants. Archaeologists have found animal bones and spear points in places where these hunters lived.

In the early 1800s, the bones of mastodons and other ancient animals were found in an area south of St. Louis. This area is known as the Kimmswick Bone Bed. It is the site of Mastodon State Park. Other evidence of our first settlers is found at Graham Cave State Park in central Missouri. In this cave were fireplaces, tools, utensils, and even sewing needles. The cave provided shelter and protection from the weather. While the men were out hunting, the women searched for plant foods, tended children, made clothing, and prepared food. Graham Cave is especially important because it shows a change from a nomadic life to one in which people stayed in one place for a longer time. Farming cannot begin unless people remain in one place.

Our First Farmers

Missouri's earliest farmers were the people of the Hopewell culture, who lived twelve hundred to fourteen hundred years ago. The Hopewells grew corn and beans and hunted small animals. One of the largest Hopewell sites is located in Saline County at Van Meter State Park. Later the Mississippi people built cities and towns along the Missouri and Mississippi rivers. About a thousand years ago, these people developed a large metropolitan center in the area of Cahokia and St. Louis. Their culture spread throughout the Mississippi and Missouri river valleys and into Arkansas, Oklahoma, and Nebraska. The Mississippi people knew how to farm well and grew large quantities of food. They were also hunters and traders. Since they lived close to the Mississippi River, fishing was an important activity. The women made handsome pots, some in animal shapes, and dinnerware decorated with symbols.

The development of towns and agriculture led to the growth of other Native American cultures. The Oneota culture, from which the Missouri tribe developed, produced excellent hunters of deer, elk, turkey, and bison, or buffalo. Fishing, gardening, and gathering were essential to the tribe's existence.

Food from the Land

When historians and archaeologists write about Native American food, they often refer to corn, squash, and beans. These three foods were the basis of North and South American Indian diets. Squash was cultivated by Native Americans before corn and beans.

Native Americans were experts at living off the land. Missouri's rivers and streams teemed with fish. The land was home to ducks, geese, deer, elk, and bison. The woods contained berries, roots, and nuts. Acorns, for example, are plentiful in Missouri, and Native Americans used them in stews or ground them into meal. They ate sunflower seeds, both raw and roasted, and they learned to make oil from the seeds for cooking and for hair dressing. Cattails were a valuable food source because all parts of the plant could be eaten—from the new shoots to the spikes and the roots.

When the weather and the hunting were good, Native Americans had plenty of food. But there were times when food was scarce. To preserve meat for the winter months, Native Americans dried and smoked game over a wooden frame set over a low fire. They made a food called pemmican, which was dried and pounded meat mixed with animal fat and crushed berries. The pemmican prevented starvation during a long winter and provided vitamins and protein. It was also taken on long hunting trips. Another kind of preserved meat was jerky, from the Spanish word *charquí*. During a hunt, some of the fresh-killed meat was sliced thin, rubbed with salt, and rolled up in an animal skin to absorb the salt and release its juices. The meat was then dried in the sun. Jerky was hard, chewy, and long lasting. The jerky found in stores today originated with Native American hunters. Corn and beans were also dried for the winter months.

Succotash is a stew of corn and beans and sometimes fish and game. The name *succotash* is a variation of an Indian word. The ingredients of this stew varied from region to region, but all contained corn and beans. The European settlers, both in the South and in New England, also prepared succotash. This meal provided a good source of protein and other important nutrients.

Native Americans used Missouri's wild plants and berries not only for food but also for soaps, dyes, and medicines. They used elderberries for tonics. They mashed the root of the curly dock plant to make a salve for sores, and they mashed the leaves, mixed them with salt, and put this "medicine" on their foreheads to treat headaches.

Osage women preparing food. (From *Indians and Archaeology of Missouri,* by Carl H. and Eleanor F. Chapman)

The Osage and Missouri

The Osage and Missouri were the major tribes in Missouri. Other tribes living in the state were the Delaware, Shawnee, Kickapoo, Iowa, Illinois, Piankashaw, Sauk, and Fox.

In Missouri, Osage women gathered plant foods and tended

gardens. Among the foods they gathered were persimmons and water lilies. They made a "cake" from seeded persimmons that was baked on boards held over a fire. Water lily roots were dried for later eating, and the seeds were enjoyed raw or roasted.

The main crops of the Osage were corn, squash, and beans. Corn was eaten boiled or roasted on the cob, or dried after cooking for storage. Parched corn, made from roasted mature grains, was like popcorn that didn't pop. Hominy was made by removing the corn kernel and soaking it in lye made from wood ashes. It was then boiled or dried. The women pre-served squash and pumpkins by cutting the pulp into strips and hanging them on racks to dry.

Meat preparation was also women's work. Although men were the hunters, the women cut, dried, and smoked meats. Men hunted in cycles, depending on the animals to be hunted. There were spring hunts for bear, and summer and fall hunts for buffalo and deer.

The Coming of the White Man

After the Europeans came to America, the way of life for the Native Americans was forever changed. They adopted the horse (reintroduced to the Americas by Columbus), which allowed them to take longer hunting trips and to overtake herds of animals. By the middle of the 1700s, almost all of the Plains Indian tribes owned horses. The British and French traded guns and other items with the Indians for fur pelts and animal skins. Guns changed the way Indians hunted and in-creased warfare among tribes as they competed for good hunt-ing grounds. Soon Indians lost most of their hunting grounds as white people pushed farther west and took Indian lands.

New World and Old World Foods

The land Columbus sighted in 1492, after thirty-three days at sea, was an island in the Caribbean, not the exotic Orient he had hoped to find. On his first voyage, Columbus spent three months visiting islands in the area and observing New World agriculture. At the time of his voyages, the Native Americans were using thousands of different plants as sources for food.

Most of the New World plants and animals were unknown to Columbus. Before returning to Spain, he learned about corn, beans, sweet potatoes, and chili peppers. He took these and other seeds back to Europe. On later voyages to the New World, he brought sugarcane and seeds of European plants such as melons, cucumbers, radishes, and lettuce. He also brought horses, cows, goats, pigs, and sheep to the New World. (The horse had been extinct in the Americas for ten thousand years.) Columbus couldn't guess the importance of his food discoveries. He started an exchange that widened the food choices of the world.

The Spanish explorers who came to the Americas after Columbus brought more livestock as well as their knowledge of how to raise the animals. Cattle branding, cattle drives, and roundups all originated in medieval Spain. In the New World, Indians were trained as the first cowboys by the Spanish.

The orange was one of the most important contributions of the Spanish to the Americas. It was planted in the Caribbean islands and in Florida. In exchange, the Spanish found out about chocolate, tomatoes, peppers, turkey, potatoes, and other New World foods.

All-American Corn

Archaeologists have found corn kernels in Mexican caves dating from 6600 B.C. By the time Columbus made his first voyage, native peoples had developed more than two hundred types of corn. In addition to yellow corn, "Indian" corn was blue, red, black, and pink. The kernels were sometimes striped or spotted. And the ear came in all sizes, from thumbnail size to two feet long.

Corn was the staple crop for Native American farmers. They had many uses for corn. To make pone, women spent hours pounding dried corn kernels with a wooden club or rock. The corn flour (meal) was blended with water and shaped into a cake. The cake was placed on the hot ashes of a fire and baked. Samp was another food made from corn. Cooked over an open fire, samp was a mixture of cornmeal and water, similar to a boiled cereal.

Corn played an important part in Native American celebrations and religious ceremonies. Different tribes created prayers, songs, dances, and stories based on corn.

Today the United States is the world's largest producer of corn. In a good year, the United States grows about 45 percent of the world's corn. Corn is one of the most important

Corn shocks on a Missouri farm. (Jim Roach)

food crops in the world, along with rice, wheat, and potatoes. Missouri is a major producer of corn.

The main use of corn is as feed for livestock. Most of the sweet corn found in our markets and grocery stores is grown on small farms or "truck farms."

Corn has many other uses. We are all familiar with corn oil, corn syrup, margarine made from corn oil, corn cereals, and corn whiskey. But corn is also used in paint, soap, adhesives, explosives, fabrics, paper, soft drinks, face powder, road de-icer, and diapers. Two promising new uses for corn are fuel ethanol and cornstarch-based plastics. Ethanol helps to reduce pollution, and the new plastics are less harmful to the environment than the old ones were.

Early French Settlement in Missouri

With the Spanish, the French were among the early explorers to search for riches in the New World. Louis Jolliet, a French trader, and Father Jacques Marquette, a Catholic missionary, traveled by canoe down the Mississippi River in 1673. They talked with Indians along the way who told them that the Missouri River started in the far northwest and was the route to the Pacific Ocean. This was not true, of course, but the story encouraged other explorers to travel the river.

Jolliet and Marquette never reached the mouth of the Mississippi. Another French explorer, Robert Cavelier, sieur de la Salle, made the long trip down the Mississippi to the Gulf of Mexico. He claimed the entire Mississippi valley for Louis XIV, the king of France. The land became known as the Louisiana Territory.

By the end of the 1600s, the French had explored a good part of Missouri. They began to trade with the Indians and found sources of lead and salt. Like the Spanish before them, the French hoped their discoveries would lead to great wealth.

The earliest French settlement in Missouri was near the River Des Peres, south of St. Louis. Lead was discovered far-

The Amoureaux House in Ste. Genevieve, one of the first houses built west of the Mississippi River. (Missouri Division of Tourism)

ther south in the 1720s. About 1750, Ste. Genevieve was established by French farmers and fur traders. Ste. Genevieve is the oldest permanent settlement in Missouri. It was called Misère (the French word for misery) because of its location on swampy land. African slaves were a part of this new settlement, and most of them spoke French. They worked in the lead mines west of Ste. Genevieve, as servants, and on the land.

The French traders sold guns, blankets, clothes, and jewelry to the Indians. The Indians sold furs and leather goods to the French. Most of the time, the two groups lived in peace.

French farmers and their slaves used a large common field to plant wheat, corn, cotton, melons, pumpkins, and tobacco.

Each family owned a strip of land in this field. This fertile river-bottom land was fenced to protect the crops from wild animals. Each farmer helped to maintain the fence around the field. Farmers also grew fruits, vegetables, and herbs in small gardens and orchards near their homes. Their farming practices reflected those of their homeland in northwestern France, where community labor was a tradition.

The French women were fine cooks. They cooked in fireplaces, using iron pots and long-handled skillets and utensils. They used native ingredients and borrowed cooking methods from the Indians and Africans. One example is gumbo, a stew thickened with dried and powdered sassafras leaves that are added just before serving. Gumbo was the name of the French dialect spoken by African slaves in Louisiana. It was also the name for okra, an African vegetable brought to America by black slaves. The word *gumbo* comes from Africa, where the plant is known as *ngombo* or *kingombo*.

Although French women used Indian corn in many ways, they preferred to make breads and rolls with wheat flour from France. So wheat flour was imported from Europe until wheat became a common crop in the New World. "French toast" comes from those early days. The cook dipped her stale bread in milk and eggs and fried it in butter.

The French settlers celebrated many religious feast days and family events. Food and drink played an important part in celebrations on Christmas, New Year's Eve, Shrove Tuesday, and Easter Sunday. A feast called *le réveillon* took place after midnight mass on Christmas. During *le réveillon*, it was traditional to serve thirteen desserts—twelve for the apostles and one for Christ.

A French New Year's Celebration

New Year's Eve was a special time for the French settlers. The young men dressed in costumes, put on masks or blackened their faces, and walked through town carrying sacks or baskets. They went from house to house, singing the song "La Guignolée." Their neighbors gave them coffee, maple syrup, eggs, meat, and other foods. Here is part of their song:

> Good evening master and mistress,
> And every one who lives here too,
> Now for the last day of the year
> La Guignolée to us is due.
> If you should be willing now,
> To give a small treat,
> We're only asking you for
> Just a very little meat.

On Epiphany, January 6, the young men shared the foods from New Year's Eve during a feast prepared by the young women.

The Establishment of St. Louis

After a long war in Europe, France turned the Louisiana Territory over to Spain in 1762. Around this time, a French merchant named Pierre Laclede and his thirteen-year-old clerk, Auguste Chouteau, came up the Mississippi River from New Orleans. They found a good site on the river for a trading post. The young Chouteau supervised the building of the post and some log houses. Laclede called this village St. Louis for the patron saint of Louis XV of France.

St. Louis soon became a busy and important trading center. Keelboats, canoes, and other boats stopped at St. Louis. The frontier town supplied more fur pelts than any other market in the world.

Meriwether Lewis and William Clark began their expedition to the West in St. Louis. In 1804, the two explorers and their men set off in three boats up the Missouri River. They traveled overland and across the Rocky Mountains to the Pacific Ocean. They recorded in their journals everything they saw along the way, from plants and animals to Indian tribes. After traveling more than four thousand miles, Lewis and Clark returned to St. Louis in 1806.

River travel increased after the first steamboat came to St. Louis in 1817. Steamboats provided regular service to the

St. Louis as seen from the Illinois shore in the mid-1800s.

town and opened up the area to a population boom. St. Louis became a stopping-off point for wagon trains heading for the West. In 1830, St. Louis had a population of about 6,000. It was still a small town. By the start of the Civil War in 1861, the town had become a city of 161,000.

The south entrance of Soulard Market, 1929. (Missouri
Historical Society)

The Soulard Market is a famous St. Louis landmark. It is
located south of the downtown area. Named for Antoine
Soulard, an early French settler, the market opened in 1779.
Local farmers came to the market in horse-drawn wagons.
They put their wagons in a circle, with the horses in the
middle, and sold their goods to people living nearby. The
term *wagon stand* comes from this early market practice.

Soulard's wife, Julia, gave the land to the city of St. Louis
in 1842, seventeen years after her husband's death. She said
that the land must always be used as a public market. The
market building was built in the 1840s and enlarged with a
market hall in 1865. A tornado destroyed the buildings in

1896. The market was soon rebuilt with new sheds. It was later improved, and by 1929 the main building and its four wings were completed. The main building was inspired by the design of a building in Florence, Italy.

Today Soulard Market is an exciting place to visit. It draws people from all over the city to buy fresh fruits and vegetables, flowers, fish, spices, baked goods, and even live chickens and geese. Many merchant and farm families have sold their produce at the market for generations. They represent a variety of cultures.

Soulard Market is said to be the oldest public market west of the Mississippi River. It is open year-round.

Becoming a State

Spain traded the Louisiana Territory back to France in 1799 in exchange for French territory in Europe. Napoleon was the ruler of France, and he decided to sell the Louisiana Territory to the United States. President Thomas Jefferson bought this land in 1803 for $15 million in what is known as the Louisiana Purchase. Eventually the states of Louisiana, Arkansas, Missouri, Nebraska, North and South Dakota, Oklahoma, and much of Kansas, Minnesota, Colorado, Montana, and Wyoming were created from this huge territory.

In the early 1800s, new settlers came to Missouri, most of them from Kentucky, Tennessee, North Carolina, and Virginia. They heard about the good, cheap land in Missouri. Daniel Boone, the famous pioneer, was one of these settlers. He and his wife, Rebecca, came to Missouri in 1799, joining one of his sons who lived near Femme Osage in the St. Charles district. Other members of the Boone family followed Daniel and Rebecca to Missouri.

After Lewis and Clark returned from their explorations of the West in 1806, more people heard about the land west of the Mississippi. Steamboats and covered wagons brought thousands of people to St. Louis and other river towns. The settlement of the West was beginning.

The Lewis and Clark expedition leaving St. Charles, May 21, 1804, on its voyage of discovery. It returned two years later. (St. Charles County Historical Society)

In 1821, Missouri achieved statehood. It entered the union as a slave state. At this time, Missouri's population was about 67,000. Missouri enjoyed a population boom after it became a state. From 1830 to 1860, the state grew from 140,000 to more than a million people. By the time of the Civil War, all but one of the state's present 114 counties had been established.

Other new residents were immigrants from northern and western Europe. The largest number of immigrants came from Germany. Some wanted religious or political freedom. Others came to escape starvation in the old country. And still others came to buy land for farming. Between 1820 and 1870, almost 2.5 million Germans emigrated to the United States.

Frontier Life

When pioneers found the land they wanted, they cut down trees and made log cabins. Their homes were simple and functional. The kitchen was the most important room in the cabin. Sometimes it was the only room. It had a dirt or a board floor, a fireplace for heating and cooking, and a few pieces of homemade furniture.

Pioneers grew corn, cotton, and other fruits and vegetables. They raised pigs and cows for food and sheep for wool. The men hunted and fished, sometimes joining Native Americans on their hunting trips. Women spent their days cooking, spinning, weaving, sewing, making candles, and caring for children.

Getting food to the table was no easy job. A fire was kept burning all the time. Meals were simple because cooking over a fire took a long time. Women cooked soups and stews in heavy iron pots. At first, these pots hung from a lug pole, which was a piece of green wood. The wood didn't last long and had to be replaced before it snapped and spilled the food into the fire. When blacksmiths came to an area, they made iron cranes for hanging pots over a fire. The pots could be raised or lowered with a system of hooks called a trammel. To roast meat, the cook tied a large piece with a rope and hung it

A Missouri frontier scene from the 1820s.

over the fire. Later, cooks used jacks and spits to turn the meat to all sides. Kitchen utensils had long handles to protect the cook's hands from the fire.

Most of us eat bread every day. Even in the smallest town, we can find white, rye, oat, or pumpernickel bread in the store. For Missouri's pioneers, making bread was a major chore, starting with the grinding of corn. Without a nearby mill, settlers had to grind their own grain. They crushed grain by hand with a mortar and pestle, or between two heavy stones called querns. Then the cook needed lard or butter, milk, water, and salt. To get these ingredients, someone had to milk a cow, fetch some water from a spring or stream, and chop wood for a fire. Lard was usually available from winter butchering, and settlers churned their own butter. The bread dough was sometimes placed on a flat, long-handled "peel" and baked on oven bricks. Or the cook baked bread in an iron pot with a heavy lid.

Americans have been great meat eaters from the time of early settlement to the present day. Today Americans eat one third of the world's meat. Many Europeans who visited the

Game birds, such as this turkey, provided good eating for early settlers. Wild turkey is still abundant in Missouri today. (Missouri Department of Conservation)

British colonies and the young United States were surprised at how much meat and liquor the Americans consumed.

Early settlers in Missouri raised cattle as a source of milk, cream, and cheese. Since milk is a fragile food and difficult to keep fresh, the settlers used naturally "soured" milk for drinking and cooking. They kept chickens for meat and eggs. But they ate more pork because it was easier to preserve than other meats. They smoked, dried, and pickled hog meat and made lard from hog fat. Game was a common meat because it was easy to come by. Salt was obtained by evaporating saltwater or brine from natural salt springs, also known as salt licks. The Boonslick region is named for the salt lick near Boonville, operated by Daniel Boone's sons in the early nineteenth century. Around this time, settlers paid $2.00 to $2.50 for a fifty-pound bushel of salt.

Although pioneer families had plenty to eat, their diets were limited by the seasons. Meat was "fried out," packed in jars, and covered with lard or tallow for long keeping. Chickens were fried when young; fat old hens were baked and tough roosters stewed. Game was always available, but fresh fruits and vegetables were usually eaten in season. Fruits and herbs were dried for the winter months. Root vegetables were stored in bins or cellars for the winter. Various fruits and vegetables were pickled or preserved with salt brine or sugar. Home canning began after the Mason jar was invented in the 1850s.

In the 1800s, life was hard for people living in the country, but country people were creative in finding ways to combine work and play. One example was barn raising. When farmers needed a new barn for animals, hay, and equipment, they called on their neighbors to help with the building. A barn raising was also an occasion for families to visit with neighbors and enjoy good food prepared by the farmwomen. People also combined work and play when they needed to husk corn, make molasses, and butcher hogs, or by holding events such as quilting bees and county fairs.

A special country event was the box supper. Young women loaded a box with their best foods, and young men called out bids for each box. Box suppers often became a time for courtship. If a young man wanted to meet a certain young woman, he would try to buy her "supper in a box."

A well-known song poked fun at church gatherings. Here is one version of the song known as "Methodist Pie":

> I went to the camp-meetin' t'other afternoon,
> To hear them shout and sing.
> And tell each other how they love one another
> And to make hallelujah ring.
> They all went there to have a good time,
> And eat the grub so sly,
> Apple sauce, butter, sugar in the gourd,
> And a great big Methodist pie.
> —Vance Randolph, *Ozark Folksongs* (University
> of Missouri Press, 1980), vol. 2

People still come from miles around to attend church suppers and county fairs. These are times when cooks show off their baked goods, with tables of cakes, fruit pies, and the preserved fruits and vegetables from their gardens. At county fairs, judges give prizes for the "best" foods.

Mills

When I go to mill I allers tie my mule up an' while I'm waitin' fer my meal, I take my gun an' dogs an' go up on the hill an' shoot a few squirrels, or else I go down an' sit on the river bank an' fish a while.

—A. O. Weaver, *Pioneers of the Ozarks*

In pioneer days, and well into the twentieth century, gristmills dotted the Missouri countryside. Many mills were found in the Ozarks, where the fast rivers and springs provided power to run the wheels. Small towns grew up around the mills. They offered services such as blacksmiths and general stores for the people who traveled long distances to the mills. Country people, sometimes entire families, made trips to the mills several times a year or after harvest time. They brought sacks of grain to be ground into flour and meal or into feed for animals. The mills became social centers where people gathered to visit with distant neighbors. One mill in Douglas County even had a barbershop where a man could get a haircut for twenty-five cents in the early part of the twentieth century.

Large waterwheels powered the mills. Later, water turbines

Wright's Mill in Miller County near the Saline Valley, in the early 1900s. (Helen Lawson)

replaced waterwheels as the main power source for mills. The actual grinding was done with stones, some weighing thousands of pounds. Many mill owners imported their stones from the mountains of France. In 1851, a miller in Iron County paid $1,000 for two French stones together weighing about three thousand pounds. Country mills produced "stone-ground flour." It was a brown, coarse, and healthful flour.

The white flour most of us use today resulted from the invention of rotary millstones with rollers. In the 1880s, all of the big milling companies in Minneapolis were using porcelain rollers. These rollers made a fine-textured flour. To make the flour white, the mills used a bleaching process. This white flour came to symbolize high quality and purity. It also lasted longer than brown flour. Bakers liked the white flour because breads and pastries made from this flour had a light and refined texture. However, the new milling processes removed the important germ and bran from wheat kernels. With the discovery of vitamins, the milling companies began adding the missing B vitamins to "enrich" their white flour.

Most of Missouri's mills closed by the middle of the twentieth century. It was easier to buy flour in grocery stores. Some of these old mills are popular tourist attractions today.

Country Ham

Nothing helps scenery like ham and eggs.

—Mark Twain

Pork was the meat of choice for Missouri's early settlers. Pigs were easy to raise, and their meat was easy to preserve. They were fattened up on corn, the main crop of the settlers.

Settlers from the southern states brought their tradition of salting and curing pork to Missouri. German immigrants also preserved pork. They used more spices and made different pork products than did their southern neighbors. Settlers often built their homes near salt springs. This assured a steady supply of the salt needed for meat preservation.

Missouri is one of several states that has an ideal climate for meat curing. The meat needs temperatures that are cold—but not too cold—to prevent spoilage during butchering and curing. Butchering was a family or community activity, held in December or January.

For the settlers, all parts of the hog had a use. For example, the "innards" (liver, kidney, intestines) were used for sausages or pressed meats. Small pieces of meat and choice cuts were used immediately or canned by pickling or by covering the

A country ham contest at the Boone County Fair, 1989. (David Pulliam, *Columbia Daily Tribune*)

cooked meat with lard. The large pieces—hams and bacons—were cured by "salting down" and smoking them over a wood fire. Then they were hung to "age." Salting a piece of pork is an old tradition. Modern curing is done with a mixture of sugar and salt.

A country ham has dark red flesh, a dry texture, and a salty flavor. This aged meat keeps for a year or more. It is very different from the pink "city hams" found in supermarkets. A favorite country dish is ham with redeye gravy and biscuits. Redeye gravy is made from ham juices, flour, a little water, and black coffee.

Missouri is famous for its country hams. Burger's Smokehouse in California, Missouri, sells more than 200,000 country hams each year. It is one of the largest country ham businesses in the United States.

An Apple a Day

In 1991, the Stark Brothers Nurseries and Orchards in Louisiana, Missouri, celebrated its 175th anniversary. This company, started by a pioneer from Kentucky, is known and respected across the United States. It is the largest family-owned fruit-tree nursery in the world. It is also one of only fifteen active companies officially incorporated by the state for more than one hundred years.

In 1816, James Hart Stark traveled from Kentucky, crossed the Mississippi River, and settled in northeast Missouri. He brought with him a bundle of apple cuttings from his father's farm. After clearing land for an orchard, Stark grafted the cuttings onto wild crab apple trees. These trees produced some of the first cultivated fruit west of the Mississippi. Stark soon became recognized for his excellent fruit and fruit trees. People traveled from many states to buy Stark trees. The Starks were also pioneers in advertising their products in newspapers, magazines, and picture catalogs.

The Stark family worked with Luther Burbank, the famous horticulturist, to introduce new varieties of fruit. By the end of the nineteenth century, Stark Brothers sold almost fifty varieties of apples.

The Starks were searching for a better apple, and in 1892

An early Stark Brothers advertisement. (Stark Bro's Nurseries)

they held a contest for the best new apple. The first prize went to a red apple from Iowa that had five bumps on its blossom end. It was named "Delicious" in honor of its fine flavor. The Stark's Delicious apple became a best-seller, earning great profits for growers.

In 1914, one of the Starks received a box from a West Virginia farmer. The box held three yellow apples. The Starks named the apples "Golden Delicious" and now market them worldwide.

Today the Delicious is the most popular apple in the United States. Almost 40 percent of the world's apples are direct descendants of the Delicious. The Golden Delicious is the second most popular apple in the United States. It represents 20 percent of all apples grown in the world.

Stark Nurseries continues to seek out new fruit varieties. It has developed many varieties of peaches, cherries, strawberries, and other fruits.

Another Missourian, Charles Bell, became well known for his apples. Bell developed the "Lady" apple at his apple orchard in Boonville. At the beginning of the twentieth century, he was often called the "Apple King of Missouri."

Settling the Ozarks

Clear streams, wooded valleys, and gentle hills make the Ozarks one of Missouri's most beautiful regions. Until modern times, the Ozarks terrain allowed for a quiet life on the land and independence from outside influences. Today we think of the Ozarks as a vacation land and a retirement haven. Tourism and retirement communities have brought many changes to the Ozarks and improved its economy. To some Ozarkers, these changes have not been for the better.

The first Ozarks settlers came in the early nineteenth century from the mountains and hills of Kentucky, Tennessee, Virginia, and the Carolinas. They were originally from England, Scotland, Wales, and Ireland. Later, Germans and other Europeans moved to the region. Settlement was gradual and in small groups, unlike the large immigrant migrations to the cities.

The Ozarks hills reminded the first settlers of their homes in the Appalachian Mountains. Although the term *backwoodsman* was used to make fun of hill people, it was a good description of where they lived—back in the woods.

The Ozarks hill people were "hardscrabble farmers," trying to scratch a living from poor soil. Since they lived far from other families and towns, these homesteaders became skilled

Molasses making in the Ozarks. (Missouri State Archives)

at living off the land. Hunting and fishing were necessary for survival. Luckily, the land and waters provided abundant food. The Ozarkers gathered native grasses, greens, and herbs to season their foods or to use for medicine. They made a "beer" from wild ginger root, a tea from sassafras leaves, and a sweetener from sorghum. The woods offered tasty berries, nuts, and many types of mushrooms. Hunters killed deer, opossums, squirrels, turkeys, ducks, and geese. The Ozarkers' taste for 'possum, raccoon, and squirrel, which they roasted or made into stews, came from their pioneer roots. They learned to "make do" with what the land offered.

Like most rural Missourians, the Ozarkers raised corn. They also grew potatoes, beans, squash, and root vegetables. They ate chicken and sometimes beef, but their main meat was pork. Pigs were set loose on the land to forage for food. Their ears were notched so their owners could find them. Each

The packing crate label used by the Ozark Fruit Growers Association, 1929. Most strawberries grown in the Ozarks were shipped to St. Louis or other cities in the eastern United States. (Missouri State Archives)

owner's identification was noted in a "Book of Brands and Notches" kept at the county courthouse.

When cool weather set in, it was time for the annual hog killing, a big event in the lives of Ozarks families. Neighbors helped each other during this time. Pork was so well liked and easy to prepare that some Ozarks people ate the meat three times a day.

Most Ozarks bread was plain and filling. The women made corn bread, corn pone, and biscuits. These breads were baked in a skillet over a fire. Yeast bread was called "fine bread" or "light bread" and was not in the tradition of the Ozarkers. (In the old country, their ancestors had baked breads in skillets or on hearthstones.) Their baking habits changed when stoves replaced hearth cooking, when white flour and commercial yeast became common, and when baking soda and baking powder became available in the mid-1800s.

Fried chicken, country ham, gravy, wilted lettuce, and corn bread—all of these "country foods" became popular for a reason. Women had busy lives and little time for fancy cooking. Instead, they favored quick cooking methods, like frying. Since there was no reliable refrigeration, they had to preserve seasonal fruits and vegetables for the winter. Pork was the meat that kept best, and its fat could be used in baking. Nothing that was grown or gathered was wasted.

As the population of the Ozarks increased, many farmers began growing fruits and vegetables on a commercial scale. The Ozarks soil was suited to the growing of apples, strawberries, peaches, and tomatoes. Between 1910 and 1940, thousands of acres were used for fruit production. Orchards of forty to a hundred acres were common. The Ozarks became known as the "Land of the Big Red Apple." Ozarks farmers organized fruit growers' associations to market their products and to obtain labor for the harvest.

Lederer's Fruit Store in Springfield, 1910. (Missouri State Archives)

In 1829, Tennessee pioneers staked a claim to a site in the Missouri Ozarks. More people followed, and in 1833 the settlement was named Springfield. These early settlers came from Kentucky, Tennessee, and Virginia. Springfield grew at a steady pace. Later settlers came from Ohio, Indiana, and New England.

Agriculture has always been important in the economy of Springfield. The railroad stimulated farm production in the Ozarks, making it easier for farmers to ship their goods to markets in other states. The Springfield city market became a showcase for Ozarks farm products. Cattle, tobacco, horses, mules, fruit, and wood were bought, sold, or traded at the market. The city became a major center to market wool, cotton, and grain.

Agricultural Fairs

Most farmers are interested in what other farmers grow and how they raise certain crops. They are especially interested in new farming equipment and practices. In the early 1820s, a group of farmers—the "planters of Missouri"—met in St. Louis to exchange information. They formed an association called the Agricultural Society of the County of St. Louis. In 1824, this group held the first agricultural fair in Missouri.

Other county fairs began in the 1830s. Farmers in Boone County exhibited their livestock in 1835. The counties of Pettis, Cooper, and Saline held fairs in 1839. Not long after, the state legislature incorporated the Missouri State Agriculture Society. This society was to educate farmers about new methods of farming. With money from the legislature, the society opened the first "state fair" in 1853 in Boonville. Two more statewide fairs were also held in Boonville.

In 1868, African Americans in Kirkwood and Carondelet sponsored a Freedmen's Fair to pay for schools and churches in the St. Louis area. Beginning in the 1870s, African Americans held their own agricultural fairs in some counties.

The county and state fairs offered farmers a chance to display and sell their goods. Farmers could also meet other farmers to talk about their work. As the number of farms grew and

41

Showing off hogs at a Missouri county fair. (Missouri State Archives)

farming became more complicated, farmers started new organizations. These organizations represented different kinds of farming like fruit growing, livestock breeding, and beekeeping.

In 1899, the Missouri legislature passed a law calling for an annual state fair. The lawmakers provided $15,000 for buildings on the fairgrounds. The location of the fair was decided by open bidding. Sedalia's bid was accepted, and it became the official state-fair city. The first fair in Sedalia, held September 9–13, 1901, was a great success. There were nineteen

Pettis County's grain and vegetable display at the Missouri State Fair, circa 1910–1920. (Missouri State Archives)

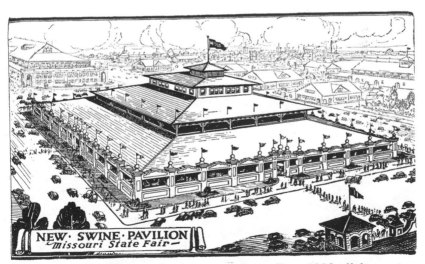

The Swine Pavilion at the Missouri State Fair, 1922. (Missouri State Archives)

buildings, including cattle and sheep barns, and a race track. A special event was an automobile that performed "fancy track work."

Every year the state fair grew in popularity. Singers, dancers, contests, fireworks, horse racing, and carnival rides added to the fun. New exhibits and buildings, like the Women's Building, attracted more people to the fair.

Today the state fair brings thousands of people to Sedalia every August. But its purpose remains the same—to demonstrate the importance of Missouri agriculture.

The Germans Come to Missouri

In the 1830s, many people in Germany read a book about Missouri written by Gottfried Duden. Duden lived in Warren County, Missouri, from 1824 to 1827. His book led some Germans to believe that Missouri was a land of easy riches. German immigrants soon found that life on the Missouri frontier was more like being in a wilderness. Many called Duden "der Lügenhund," which means a lying dog.

Some Germans came to Missouri in the early 1800s from North Carolina and other states, but the majority of German immigrants came later. Some traveled from eastern ports overland and then by steamboat on the Ohio and Mississippi rivers to St. Louis. Others came from New Orleans to St. Louis by steamboat. They settled in St. Louis or moved westward into the new state. Two early German settlements were Westphalia and Hermann. Westphalia, in central Missouri, was settled in 1835 by people from the Westphalia area of Germany. Hermann is on the Missouri River about a hundred miles west of St. Louis. It was named after a German war hero who defeated the Roman soldiers in A.D. 9.

The people who founded Hermann in 1837 were new im-

Outdoor beer gardens were favorite gathering places for Missouri's German immigrants who enjoyed the beer, food, and music. This photo from 1880 shows Schnaider's beer garden in St. Louis. (State Historical Society of Missouri)

migrants from Philadelphia. Their town and the surrounding area reminded the settlers of their homeland, especially the area along the Rhine River. Today the area is known as the Missouri Rhineland. Soon the Germans were planting grapes for wine making. The Germans brought new foods and new ways of cooking to Missouri. Along with the British, the Germans have had a great influence on American food.

Like the French, the Germans were good cooks and gardeners, and they enjoyed eating. Germans were fond of potatoes. They had grown them in the old country since the 1700s, when Frederick the Great of Prussia encouraged the people in his kingdom to plant potatoes. The Germans who settled on farms in Missouri planted potatoes from the beginning. They made delicious meals from this simple food. Potatoes were boiled, steamed, fried, and coated with herbs and vinegar. They were made into crispy pancakes, dumplings, salads, and even chocolate cake. We can thank the Germans for their potato salad, one of America's favorite summer and picnic foods. Germans liked a sweet-sour taste in many of their foods. This combination gave foods a sharp, spicy taste. It was a change from the plain foods pioneer Americans ate at the time.

The food most of us know as German is the sausage, or wurst. Germans have been making sausage since the Middle Ages. Sausage is made in all European countries, wherever beef or pork is available. But the Germans make more sausage than any other nationality. Many sausages took their names from towns in Germany or Austria. For example, *wienerwurst* means Vienna sausage. We use the term *wiener* today to mean a frankfurter, named after the German town of Frankfurt. Also named for places are braunschweiger (Brunswick), made from liver and pork, and thuringer (Thuringia), which is summer sausage. Among the sausages that came from Germany are knockwurst, mettwurst, weisswurst, blutwurst, bockwurst, and bratwurst.

Another food we associate with Germans is the hamburger. The hamburger came to Germany from Russia. It came to Russia from central Asia, where it was eaten by Tartar warriors as a patty of raw meat. Seamen introduced this "Tartar steak" to people in the port city of Hamburg. This dish later became known as "Hamburg steak" and was brought to America by German immigrants.

Sauerkraut is also a famous dish thought to be of German origin. But it, too, came from Asia. Workers who were building the Great Wall in China in 200 B.C. ate chopped cabbage marinated in rice wine. Like hamburger, this dish traveled to Russia and was brought to Germany by seamen. During World War I, when there was much prejudice against Germans in America, sauerkraut was renamed "Liberty Cabbage."

Germans became well-known cheese makers in America,

but most of the cheese-making Germans settled in the dairy state of Wisconsin. Today the United States is the world's largest cheese-making country. Many of our cheeses originated in Germany or were adapted by Germans from the cheeses of other European countries such as France, England, Italy, the Netherlands, and Switzerland.

Germans often opened bakeries when they moved to a city or town. These bakeries became meeting places for both old and new immigrants. It was the Germans who gave us some of our most delicious sweets and breads. Germany is the home of the jelly doughnut, a popular breakfast food across the United States. In Germany, the jelly doughnut is called a *Berliner Pfannkuchen,* or sometimes a *Bismarck.* Bakers make this doughnut as a special treat for Shrove Tuesday, the day before Lent begins. Other baked goods from the Germans include apple strudel, fruit fritters, stollen (coffee cake), kaiser rolls, pretzels, rye and pumpernickel breads, and many kinds of cookies.

A German Christmas in Missouri

Christmas food customs in Germany were different in each region. A German immigrant from Westphalia observed the Christmas season with different activities than a German from Bavaria. Missouri's German immigrants came from many regions of Germany, so their Christmas customs differed from community to community. They shared some customs in common, such as decorating an evergreen tree, going to midnight mass, and baking special cakes, breads, and cookies.

The Christmas season began early for German settlers. There was often a bonfire on the night before St. Martin's Day, November 11. Children joined street processions on St. Martin's Day. They went from house to house begging for sweets made especially for the feast day.

During Advent, the four weeks before Christmas, families prepared all kinds of treats for the holidays. On the eve of St. Nicholas Day, December 5, children left their shoes near their beds or on a windowsill. When they awakened, they found their shoes filled with candy, fruit, and cookies. St. Nicholas Day has been celebrated in Germany since the Middle Ages. It is also celebrated by people from other European countries.

The Germans introduced the custom of the Christmas tree, or *Tannenbaum*, to the United States. Americans quickly adopted this colorful and happy custom. In Missouri, German settlers cut down some of the state's many cedars for their Christmas trees.

Many Germans ate a cold salad of meat and fish on Christmas Eve or Christmas Day. This was supposed to bring good luck in the new year. But the glory of a German Christmas was the sweets. It was time to enjoy the fruits of all those weeks of baking. Some of these sweets are made today in German communities. Some are so popular and delicious that they are made by people all across the state and country.

One famous German treat is *Springerle*, an anise-flavored cookie stamped with designs of flowers, animals, and scenes. The designs are made with wooden boards or rolling pins. There are other German cookies imprinted with designs. These cookies date back to pagan times. Another delicious cookie is *Pfeffernuss*, or "pepper nut," a spicy ball that contains pepper. *Christstollen* is a yeast bread filled with raisins, fruits, and nuts. *Zimtsterne* are star-shaped cookies made with ground almonds and cinnamon. Many Missourians are familiar with *Lebkuchen*, a honey-spice cookie that has been "aged," sometimes for up to a month. Spices like cinnamon, cloves, cardamom, nutmeg, and anise are common to German Christmas cookies.

The Swiss Germans also have special Christmas sweets. *Leckerli* cookies are made from crushed almonds and stamped with designs. *Brunsli*, or brown cookies, contain ground almonds and chocolate. Swiss pastry chefs are well known for their beautiful and luscious treats. The Christmas season is a great time to visit a Swiss pastry shop.

Missouri Wine Making

The making of wine is an important part of Missouri's economic and cultural history. Missouri grape growers and wine makers were nationally known by the late nineteenth century.

The early French settlers made wine from native grapes, fermented cider from apples, and brandy from peaches. Pioneer women made "weed wines" from dandelions, elderberries, herbs, and fruits.

Dutzow, in Warren County, was founded in 1832 and became one of Missouri's first wine-making towns. But it was in Hermann that Missouri wine was to grow into a major industry. The hills around Hermann were well suited to grape growing. The town was also on the Missouri River, which made for easy shipping of wine.

In 1848, eleven years after Hermann was established, the town's wineries produced ten thousand gallons of wine. That same year, Hermann held its first *Weinfest*, or wine festival, with a big parade. In the 1850s, Hermann wine makers were selling wines, grape juice, and root stock to other states. By 1856, the wineries made a hundred thousand gallons of wine. Wine making slowed down during the Civil War because many Hermann men left the area to join the Union army. By the 1870s and 1880s, the wine business in Gasconade County

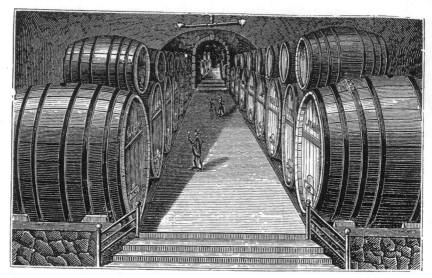

Storage Cellar No. 3 at Stone Hill Winery in Hermann in the early 1900s. Its capacity was a hundred and fifty thousand gallons. (Stone Hill Winery)

was booming again. And by the 1890s, Hermann's Stone Hill Winery was the nation's third largest.

The Germans considered wine making a respectable profession. They enjoyed wine or beer with their meals and had no taboos about drinking alcoholic beverages. Entire families gathered in *Weingärten* (wine gardens) to eat and drink. This practice was very different from that of many settlers from eastern and southern states who had religious scruples about alcohol consumption.

In the 1850s, the railroads brought more European immigrants to Missouri. Railroad companies promoted agriculture, including wine growing, along their routes. The companies sold land near the rail lines, where towns developed along with farms. Boonville was one of these railroad towns. Its winery operated between 1850 and 1880.

Many Missouri grape growers experimented with grape cuttings to develop new varieties of grapes. They sent healthy

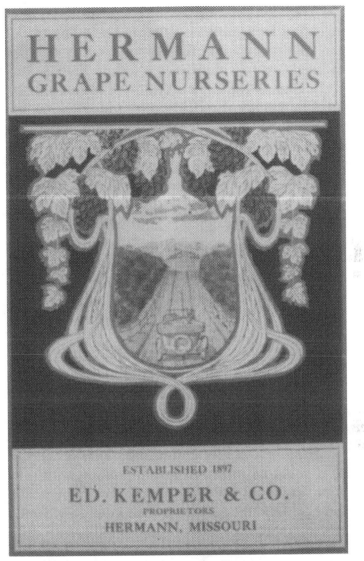

The cover of a catalog from the Kemper grape nursery in Hermann in the early 1900s. (Anna Kemper Hesse)

Missouri grape roots to France in the 1870s to replant vineyards attacked by a pest that destroyed grape roots. A Swiss-German, Hermann Jaeger of Newton County near Neosho, sent railroad cars full of grape cuttings to France. Jaeger received the cross of the French Legion of Honor for his effort.

Hermann was not the only town in which wine was king. Towns such as Altenburg, Augusta, Freeburg, Westphalia, and Wittenberg also had wineries. A group of Germans settled near Monett in southwest Missouri, where they grew wine grapes. And a group of French people went to Dillon in Phelps County, where grapes were already under cultivation by Germans.

A group of Italians bought land from the railroad near St. James in 1898. Like the Germans, Italians liked wine with their meals. They began growing grapes in 1905. They named their town for Bishop Joseph Rosati, the second Catholic bishop of St. Louis. Grapes for juice and wine are still grown in Rosati.

Missouri's wine industry grew throughout the late nineteenth and early twentieth centuries. Only California made more wine than Missouri. Before 1920, Stone Hill Winery was the second largest wine producer in the United States. Stone Hill's wines won many international awards.

The United States wine industry was almost destroyed when Congress passed the Volstead Act in 1920. Under this law, commonly known as Prohibition, no alcoholic beverages of any kind could be made or sold in the country. The only exception was wine for religious services. Wineries in Missouri and other states pulled up their grape vines and closed down. Some grape growers planted orchards, and some winery buildings were used for other purposes. Stone Hill grew mushrooms in the huge cellars of its winery until 1967.

Prohibition ended in 1933, but it took many years before American wineries started new vineyards and made wine. It wasn't until the mid-1960s that wine making began again in Missouri. Today there are more than twenty-five wineries in Missouri, making many varieties of sweet and dry wine, and even champagne.

Missouri Brewing

Beer is an ancient drink. Historians trace the brewing of beer back to the time before Christ. Beer originated in the Near East and Egypt, where it was made from barley and other grains.

In the Middle Ages, beer became a commercial product, and it was refined over the years in Europe and England. In the 1800s, German immigrants brought their brewing skills to America. They made brewing one of America's—and Missouri's—largest industries.

Americans have been drinking beer since colonial times. The first private brewery in the United States was opened by two Dutch immigrants on Manhattan Island in 1612. Beer was made from corn until new grains, like barley, were found to grow well in America. The beer we are most familiar with today is made with barley, hops, and yeast.

The brewing of Missouri beer began in the early nineteenth century. Jacques St. Vrain opened a brewery north of St. Louis in 1810. He hired Victor Habb, a German brewer, to make "strong beer" and "table beer." Several small breweries also opened around this time. St. Louis was naturally suited to brewing. It had miles of underground caves where beer could be stored. And it had plenty of river water. Beer is 97 percent water.

In 1840, Adam Lemp, a German immigrant, opened a brewery in St. Louis. Lemp began making lager beer. Most Americans were not familiar with this type of beer. It was a light beer, made with special yeasts and well aged. Lemp's Brewery was a success from the start.

Across the state, the Weston Royal Brewing Company opened in 1842. This brewery aged its beer in underground stone cellars forty, fifty, and sixty feet deep. The company advertised its product as "The Beer That Made Milwaukee Jealous."

By 1854, St. Louis had twenty-four breweries. By 1860, there were forty breweries, with an output of 189,400 gallons a year. The breweries employed hundreds of new immigrants. Beer gardens opened across the city and in other German towns. And lager beer became the standard American brew.

Adolphus Busch was only eighteen years old when he came to St. Louis in 1857. He sold brewing supplies, and one of his customers was Eberhard Anheuser. Anheuser was part owner of a struggling brewery. Busch married one of Anheuser's daughters and later joined his father-in-law's brewery. Busch was an exceptional salesman as well as a risk taker. He was the first American brewer to pasteurize beer. This allowed beer to be stored for a long time. The Anheuser-Busch brewery grew rapidly, adding new buildings and cellars. Its beer was the first to be sold nationally. Today there are Busch plants across the United States, employing thousands of people. The Busch brewery is the largest in the world.

Breweries existed in other Missouri towns and cities such as St. Joseph, Kansas City, Sedalia, Boonville, and Jefferson City. Most closed with Prohibition, although a few stayed open and produced "near beer," a nonalcoholic beverage. Some Missouri breweries reopened after Prohibition and operated until the 1960s, but they could not meet the competition from the large national breweries.

The Anheuser-Busch Brewery in St. Louis is the largest brewery in the world. (State Historical Society of Missouri)

Making beer at Boulevard Brewing Company. This Kansas City firm is one of several new micro-breweries in Missouri. (Boulevard Brewing Co.)

Today small regional breweries are opening throughout the United States. These "micro-breweries" take pride in making beer with a different taste than that of the national brands. Several micro-breweries operate in Missouri. Their beer is often unpasteurized and promoted for its freshness.

Food Preservation

Until the nineteenth century, the preservation of food had not changed much since ancient times. Food can be preserved by smoking, salting, pickling, drying, canning, and freezing. The first four methods have been used for centuries, but the last two methods were developed only in the nineteenth century.

Missouri settlers ate what they grew, but many foods could not be kept for more than a few days. Missouri's hot and humid summers caused food to spoil quickly. One answer to this problem was ice from the farm pond. Families cut ice from frozen ponds and stored it in a pit covered with straw or sawdust. Some homes had outdoor cellars or a springhouse where the cool springwater ran around cooling trays that held food. Some families even hung foods in the coolness of a well.

Tin Cans and Mason Jars

In the days before refrigeration, women preserved vegetables by pickling them in salt brine and vinegar. They dried fruits in the sun. Meat was salted down or smoked. Sometimes meat was packed in crocks or jars and covered with a thick layer of lard. Food poisoning was common from improperly preserved foods.

Inside the Billings Canning Factory in Christian County, 1920s. (State Historical Society of Missouri)

In 1809, Nicholas Appert, a Frenchman, invented canning in vacuum-packed, sealed-glass containers. He canned meat for Napoleon's armies. Appert wrote a book in 1810 called *A Book for All Housekeepers; or, The Art of Preserving All Kinds of Animal and Vegetable Substances for Several Years.* His discovery started modern food processing and led to research in canning, drying, and freezing of foods.

In 1825, sixteen years after Appert canned his first foods, a patent for tin cans was taken out by Thomas Kensett, an Englishman who lived in the United States. Before long, most food companies had changed from glass containers to tin cans. Salmon and lobster were the first commercially canned foods, followed by corn, tomatoes, and peas. Early tin cans were made by tinsmiths. A tinsmith could produce fifty to sixty cans a day. In 1849, a new machine reduced the hand labor of making cans, and an unskilled laborer could turn out 750 cans a day.

Another important discovery was made by a man named Gail Borden. He discovered how to condense milk so it could be stored and transported. His discovery, which involved evaporating whole milk in a vacuum pan, was patented in 1856. The United States government bought all of his condensed milk for soldiers fighting in the Civil War. Borden became a rich man.

The Mason jar that we still use today was patented in 1858. Its screw-top, glass-lined lid and "jar rubber" created an airtight seal to preserve the food inside the jar. Mason jars made possible the home canning of fruits, vegetables, and meats.

A tomato-canning industry developed in the Ozarks in the 1890s and lasted for about sixty years. Tomatoes grew well in the Ozarks, and there was plenty of water for the canning process. Most of the canneries were small. They helped the local economy and provided paying jobs for people living in the hills. Families often traveled miles to the canneries for the annual harvest and canning. The work was exhausting, but workers could visit with their friends and neighbors while working.

The Civil War and Food Supply

An army marches on its stomach.

—Napoleon

Missouri was a divided state in a divided nation during the Civil War. The issues of slavery and states' rights split the United States into two camps. From 1861 to 1865, the country battled over how to interpret the U.S. Constitution and Bill of Rights.

Missouri was one of five "border" states. It remained in the Union but still allowed slavery, although many people in the state opposed slavery. Missourians fought in both the Union and the Confederate armies. More than four hundred battles were fought in Missouri, many by small groups of guerrillas. The war brought great destruction to the state and its people.

At the beginning of the war, most soldiers had enough to eat. But, as the war progressed, food supplies became short, especially for Confederate soldiers.

The South was mostly an agricultural region. Its economy was based on crops, such as tobacco and cotton, that used

The camp kitchen of General John C. Fremont's dragoons at Tipton, 1861. (State Historical Society of Missouri)

slave labor. The South had few farm machines and a poor transportation system. Even though much southern land was converted from cotton to food production for the war, Confederate soldiers often had little to eat. There were shortages of salt to preserve food and of containers to ship food. Many of the railroad cars that could carry food needed repair, and so did the rails themselves. These repairs were often impossible to make. There was even a shortage of cooking kettles, skillets, and utensils.

Confederate soldiers wrote letters to their families about sickness and near starvation among the troops. Sometimes they had only flour, preserved meat, and dry corn to eat. Lack of fruit and vegetables caused scurvy and other health problems. Soldiers were lucky if there were nearby cornfields or orchards to raid. Their typical ration was cornbread and beef.

The meat was usually hard, tough, and often spoiled. Soldiers got so tired of corn bread that many vowed never to eat it after the war.

To supplement their rations, soldiers stalked and trapped small game. They knocked birds from their roosts with sticks and killed rabbits with rocks and clubs. If they were near streams, they got fish by setting out hooks or simply grabbing fish from the water. They made "coffee" from dried apples, potatoes, and peanuts. Tea was made from herbs, corn bran, and sassafras. In 1863, the Confederate army commanders authorized the slaughtering of mules for food because beef and pork were in short supply.

Both the Union troops and the Confederate soldiers and guerrillas raided Missouri's farms and towns for food and drink. In the 1980s, an Ozarks man told a family story about one of these raids to Don Love, a Missouri writer and teacher:

> Grandmother had all her provisions for winter such as molasses, preserves, corn for bread, and animals but saw them all carried away by the soldiers, and some dumped out. The big stone jar full of preserves was broken and dumped beside a big stump not far from the house. The corn cribs were made of logs and unroofed. The corn was shoveled into wagons commandeered from neighbors. As the corn lowered in the crib the logs were thrown off so there was no effort to shovel the corn in the wagons. When they reached the bottom of the crib there was no more corn and no more logs. One neighbor who was forced to use his team and wagon sat glumly on the rail fence with his back turned to the house, while the soldiers raided the crib.

Soldiers had to be creative to survive the hardships of war. When General John S. Marmaduke and his troops were on their way to join General Sterling Price in 1864, they stopped at Trautwein's Mill outside Hermann. There they found plenty of flour. Next to the mill were a number of sycamore stumps, three to four feet in diameter. Cooks used the flour to make biscuits for the troops. They used the tree stumps as tables for rolling out the biscuit dough. After the biscuits were made, the officers used those same "tables" for eating.

The Civil War was not as damaging to the northern states as it was to the southern and border states. Few battles were fought on northern soil. The North had many industries other than farming. One of these industries was canning. Many canning companies provided food for the Union army. It was easier to preserve and to ship canned food. Companies also began canning a greater variety of foods. Fruit was canned for the first time during the Civil War.

The war increased food production in the North. Farmers grew more corn and wheat and raised more livestock. Union soldiers were better fed than the Confederates. Their rations were more varied, and they had real coffee. But Union troops also suffered food shortages.

Union soldiers complained about "old bull" and pickled meat so salty it made blisters on the tongue. Their "bread" was called hardtack, or pilot biscuit. Hardtack was a cracker made from flour and water. The cracker was often stale or full of bugs. Some who ate the hardtack whole said the cracker was so hard that chewing it made their gums ache. Others said their teeth needed sharpening with a file to eat the cracker. Hardtack was often pounded into meal to make a pudding or added to stews and soups.

Despite their complaints, both sides were more concerned about the quantity of their food than its quality or preparation. Delicate appetites had no place during wartime.

The Civil War helped the emerging food-processing industry. Business people realized that new markets would open soon for canned goods. After the war, the stage was set for the growth of American food processing. New machines were invented for canning companies, and new food businesses opened across the country.

African American Food Traditions

Cornless, cornless are we
Just as cornless as cornless can be
The planters don't allow us to raise it
So cornless, cornless are we.
— John Handcox, African American
farm labor organizer in the 1930s

African Americans have lived in Missouri since the early days of settlement. Almost a third of the people in the first French communities were black. Most of them were slaves. The first blacks came, unwillingly, to the Missouri territory in 1719 to work in French lead mines. In 1720, Philippe François Renault came from France to manage lead mines in Missouri. Historians say he brought about five hundred black slaves from Haiti to Missouri. At the time of the Louisiana Purchase in 1803, blacks were 13 percent of Missouri's population. Missouri attracted new settlers with its rich land and its business opportunities in St. Louis. Missouri also allowed slavery, which encouraged settlement from the south.

A Life of Struggle

Slaves were considered property under the law. They had few rights and little personal freedom. Around 1816, a slave could be bought for a thousand dollars. Most slaves labored on farms, where they worked from dawn to dusk. Their owners provided food, housing, and clothing. Some owners allowed their slaves to tend their own gardens or to raise chickens and pigs.

Slaves received a weekly ration of corn, salt pork or bacon, molasses, fruit, and vegetables. The rations varied according to the foods grown in the area, the season, and local customs.

Owners often gave their slaves the "leavings" of pigs, chicken, or cattle. These were the intestines, head, feet, and other animal parts considered less desirable. It took more time to cook these parts, which meant even more work after a hard day of labor. One dish prepared from the leavings was chitterlings, or "chitlins," the small intestines of a pig. Chitlins had to be cooked for a long time. Then they were cut up and fried. Potatoes, grits, corn bread, and greens were other foods common among slaves.

Slaves (and "poor whites") made hoecakes from cornmeal and water. The cakes were placed on the blade of a hoe and baked over a fire. There were other quick ways to cook breads made with corn. Cracklin' bread was a tasty bread made with cornmeal and fried bits of pork skin. Ashcakes were cornbread cakes covered with ashes and baked over hot coals.

How well the slaves ate depended on their owners. Most slaves had little more than basic foods. Since slaves were not allowed to own guns, they learned clever ways to trap or to use slingshots to capture squirrels, rabbits, geese, and other game. Fish also added to their diets.

Greens were (and still are) important in the African American diet. They were cooked down with ham hocks or salt pork and seasoned with vinegar and spices. The juices from cooked greens were called "pot likker." Children and adults

Edith Cross of Jefferson City was an expert at making beaten biscuits, a regional specialty. Cross died in 1991 at the age of 103. (Missouri State Archives)

drank these nutritious juices. The Ozarks settlers also drank pot likker.

African Americans have long been known for their cooking skills. President George Washington replaced his white cook with Hercules, one of his slaves from Mount Vernon. African Americans helped to develop the Creole cooking of Louisiana. They cooked for rich families in New York, Boston, Philadelphia, and other cities. And they prepared elegant dinners for government officials in Williamsburg, Virginia, and Washington, D.C. At the "Big House" on plantations, in Missouri and throughout the South, black women cooked fine meals for their owners' families.

In their own homes, African American women developed inventive ways to cook the food available to them. They became expert at knowing by sight, sound, and feel just the right ingredients to make a dish perfect. Corn and pork were the basis for many dishes now referred to as "soul food." *Soul food* has more than one meaning. It can mean ways of cooking passed down from generation to generation. But its most common meaning is food cooked with heart and soul.

Not all of Missouri's slaves worked on farms. Some worked as carpenters, nurses, butlers, and day laborers. Owners sometimes rented their slaves to work in mines, on riverboats, and later on the railroads. There were also free blacks, but they were a small percentage of the black population. The free blacks tended to settle in St. Louis, where they worked as blacksmiths, masons, gardeners, painters, and seamstresses. Some owned businesses and were very successful. Some became well-known chefs in homes and restaurants. St. Louis was famous in the early 1800s for angel food cake, made by black cooks. Only rich people could afford this expensive cake. One cake required a dozen egg whites beaten by hand.

African Americans took part in the westward expansion. They worked as cowboys in the West and as cooks on the wagon trains journeying into new territory. During the Civil War, the Union army sometimes hired free blacks as cooks. African Americans also worked as food vendors. They visited army camps to sell fruits, vegetables, and baked goods. In the early years of the war, many Confederate soldiers used their black slaves to cook for the troops. Most slaves were sent home as food became scarcer and the need for farm labor increased.

Times of Change

After the Civil War ended in 1865, African Americans were freed, but their problems did not end. Without education, they had only a limited chance for a better life. The importance of education for African Americans was well understood by the founders of Lincoln University in Jefferson City. Lincoln was established with funds from black soldiers who fought in the Union army. The school became a training ground for teachers.

During the time of Reconstruction, some blacks continued to work for their former owners. Many migrated to cities, where they hoped to find work in the new factories. In 1879, most black males still worked on farms.

As train travel became common, the railroads hired blacks as cooks and chefs. These cooks often prepared fancy meals with expensive ingredients on first-class trains. In cities and towns, blacks opened restaurants where they served specialties such as sweet potato pie, catfish, and biscuit bread pudding.

From the late 1800s until World War I, blacks moved to the cities in large numbers. Many came up the Mississippi to settle in St. Louis and later in Kansas City. Among these new migrants were musicians. They developed a distinctive form of jazz, which enlivened the nightlife of the two cities.

A major contribution to American agriculture was made by George Washington Carver, the famous African American scientist. Carver was born into slavery in Missouri during the Civil War. After years of fighting poverty and prejudice, Carver earned many college degrees and became a teacher and researcher. He showed southern farmers how to save their soil by planting peanuts. His research on the peanut at Tuskegee Institute in Alabama resulted in more than three hundred products made from this legume—from cooking oil and paint to laxatives and printer's ink. Carver experimented with many other vegetables such as tomatoes, sweet potatoes, and cowpeas. His advice on growing these foods, and his recipes, were popular across the country.

Well into the twentieth century, the lives of African Americans were limited by the attitudes and laws of whites. Most of Missouri's black people lived in cities or developed their own rural towns. African Americans maintained rich cultural and social lives apart from whites. They built schools, churches, and businesses to serve their communities.

The church has always been a vital part of African American communities. It has provided a center for civil rights organization and community development for people of color. Churches also bring people together for social events such as church suppers. Barbecues, fish fries, and family reunions are other occasions for the enjoyment of good food among African Americans.

Today the many contributions of African Americans are no longer ignored. In one way or another, African American art, literature, and music figure in the lives of all Americans. African American food is part of this proud heritage.

People who study the origin of words believe that *barbecue* comes from the Spanish or French. In Spanish, *barbacoa* refers to a wooden rack for roasting meat or fish. In French, *barbe à queue* describes how an animal is roasted—from head to tail. During their explorations of the New World, the Spanish saw Caribbean natives grilling meat outdoors. On the Atlantic and Gulf coasts, Native Americans grilled and smoked meat, fish, and fowl on wooden racks over an outdoor fire. This practice later spread through the southern states and to the Southwest. The spicy sauces for barbecue were the contribution of the Spanish.

Americans have enjoyed eating outdoors since the days of the pioneers. On the frontier, outdoor cooking was practical on hot days. Barbecues soon became popular across the country as family get-togethers and community events.

Today barbecue is big business in restaurants. Chefs lure customers with their secret sauces. Some of these sauces have earned millions for their creators.

In the Midwest, beef, pork, and chicken are the preferred barbecue meats. Missouri has hundreds of barbecue restaurants, many operated by African Americans. It is said that barbecue reaches an art form in Kansas City. Restaurant critics give high praise to the city's barbecue.

Two popular Kansas City barbecue restaurants are Arthur Bryant's and Gates and Sons Bar-B-Q. African Americans own both establishments. Bryant's was started by Charlie Bryant in the 1930s. Charlie had worked with Henry Perry, the father of Kansas City barbecue. Charlie's brother, Arthur, took over in 1946, and the restaurant became a city institution. Bryant called his restaurant a "grease house." It was

Gates and Sons Bar-B-Q is one of Kansas City's famous barbecue establishments. (Gates Bar-B-Q)

integrated in the 1950s when few other places in the city were. Ollie Gates started his first restaurant in the 1940s. Now there are several Gates Restaurants in Kansas City, as well as a training center for workers called Gates Rib Tech.

The Transportation Revolution

Missouri's towns and cities grew rapidly in the second half of the 1800s. Part of this growth came from new businesses and factories, which brought many people from rural to urban areas. City people no longer lived close to their sources for food. Transportation of food by steamboat and later by rail opened up new markets for farmers.

In 1817, the first steamboat arrived in St. Louis. It was called the *Zebulon M. Pike*. By 1819, sixty steamboats were operating on the Mississippi River. By the 1830s, more than five hundred steamboats came to St. Louis each year. In 1819, the *Independence* became the first steamboat to travel the Missouri River. The heyday of steamboating on the Missouri River was from 1850 to 1860. These big boats, some two hundred and fifty feet long, could carry up to four hundred people and tons of freight. It cost a passenger $25.00 to travel on a steamboat from St. Louis to Kansas City.

St. Louis was an important steamboat center. In the late 1850s, more steamboats left St. Louis to travel the Missouri River than traveled on both the upper and the lower Mississippi.

Activity on steamboats docked at the St. Louis riverfront, 1874.
(State Historical Society of Missouri)

Steamboats carried settlers heading west and brought all kinds of goods to river towns—from dishes and clothes to food and mail. Steamboats also helped to create new towns.

Railroads had a major effect on food production and the American diet. In 1859, the first railroad line across Missouri was completed, running from Hannibal to St. Joseph. More railroads were built in the years before the Civil War. After the war, Missouri became crisscrossed with railroads. In 1869, the first transcontinental railroad was completed, joining the tracks of the Union Pacific and the Central Pacific in the mountains of Utah. Railroads opened up formerly isolated areas, and they connected towns and cities. New towns grew up around railroad stops. The railroads also isolated those areas they bypassed.

As rail transportation became cheaper, food became cheaper. Railroads enabled farmers to ship their grain and produce to new markets. The farmers' surplus food could be sold in city markets, bringing variety to city dwellers' meals. The rail-

THE KATY FLYER
..BETWEEN..
St. Louis,
Chicago,
Kansas City

AND

MISSOURI,
KANSAS,
THE INDIAN TERRITORY,
OKLAHOMA,
TEXAS,
MEXICO AND
CALIFORNIA POINTS.

C. HAILE,
Traffic Manager.

JAMES BARKER,
General Passenger and Ticket Agent.

ST. LOUIS, MO.

Advertisement for the KATY Railroad, early 1900s.

roads brought food from both coasts to the Midwest. Fruits grown on the West Coast reached midwestern and eastern tables in good condition.

The first cattle to ride the rails—twenty carloads—left Abilene, Kansas, in 1867. Cattle that rode to market instead of walking had less weight loss and produced tender meat. Before trains, pigs walked to market. When this was no longer necessary, new breeds were developed for meat with more flavor and tenderness.

The railroads increased the kinds and quality of food available to Missourians. Railroads also spurred the development of new food stores in all parts of the country. By the dawn of the twentieth century, foods available in one part of the country were available in all parts of the country.

Destroying the Buffalo

A sad chapter in American history concerns the destruction of the buffalo. Early explorers saw millions of buffalo roaming the plains. Some reports put the number at 60 million; others say 100 million.

The buffalo was the main source of meat for Native Americans in the Midwest and the West. But meat was not the only use for the buffalo. The animal's hide and sinews were used for clothes, tepees, saddles, and bowstrings. Its hair was made into rope, its stomach into food containers, its horns into spoons, its tendons into thread. Buffalo chips were burned for cooking fuel and heating.

Most white people had little interest in eating buffalo meat. But there was a market for buffalo tongues—a delicacy—in eastern restaurants and in Europe. So thousands of buffalo were killed for their tongues, which were smoked and shipped to luxury markets. Buffalo robes were popular in the early to mid-1800s. For this special market, 67,000 buffalo pelts were shipped to St. Louis in 1840.

Buffalo interfered with cattle raising and with the railroads. They were wild animals and competed with cattle for pasture. They got in the way of railroad cars. Some railroads had special trains for hunters. The hunters shot at buffalo

from train windows. Later the railroads hired professional hunters to kill buffalo. Buffalo Bill Cody was one of those hired hunters. It is claimed he killed 4,280 buffalo in one year.

Another reason for killing the buffalo was to force Native Americans off their land. The Homestead Act, passed by Congress in 1863, promised free land to new settlers. Whites began moving westward onto Native American lands. Native Americans feared losing their hunting grounds. Without their main food source—the buffalo—Native Americans began waging war on white communities for food. The army protected white settlers by fighting Native Americans.

President Ulysses S. Grant vetoed a bill to save the buffalo in 1875. In the end, Native Americans saw some of their treaties with the government broken, most of their land taken, and their lives changed as they were forced to live on reservations.

By the start of the twentieth century, the only buffalo on the North American continent were found in Yellowstone Park (where there were only twenty-one) and in Canada (where there was a small herd). Today, buffalo herds are increasing in the western states. Buffalo can be found in many zoos, and even on some Missouri farms. Buffalo meat is also appearing on restaurant menus as a new "gourmet" food.

The Growth of Kansas City

One of Kansas City's best-known landmarks is a statue of a Native American scout, located on a hill in Penn Valley Park. The scout is looking toward the vast plains that helped Kansas City grow into a great midwestern metropolis.

Native Americans lived in the Kansas City area before a town was established. They engaged in fur trading with white people. In the mid-1800s, the Indians moved farther west. More white settlers came by steamboat to the area. Many were on their way to the Far West, but others stayed. They discovered there was money to be made, supplying farmers and travelers with goods and services.

The town of Independence was established in 1827. Westport, now a part of Kansas City, was incorporated in 1833. It was to be the site of a major Civil War battle. The town of Kansas was founded in 1839. It was incorporated in 1850, changed its name to the City of Kansas in 1853, and changed it again to Kansas City in 1889. Along with St. Joseph and Independence, Kansas City was a busy place in the mid-1800s. The Santa Fe and Oregon trails brought thousands of people to the area, where they prepared for their overland journeys. Supplying the wagon trains became big business for local outfitters.

The bridge over the Missouri River that helped make Kansas City a major transportation center.

With the coming of the railroads, Kansas City changed from a frontier town to a leading commercial hub. St. Joseph had hoped to become the major western Missouri city. But St. Joseph had no bridge over the Missouri River. Kansas City built a bridge over the river in 1869 and soon became an important transportation and agricultural center. Meatpacking plants and flour mills were built to process the cattle and grain shipped to the city. The city's population increased as the new industries grew.

In 1856, the Kansas City Board of Trade was organized by a group of Kansas City merchants. Today the board is the world's most important marketplace for wheat. Board members gather daily to buy and sell wheat "futures." A future is a contract between a buyer and a seller to make or take delivery of a product at a future date. The contract guarantees price, quantity, and time of delivery. Prices set in Kansas City influence wheat prices all over the world.

Kansas City had only one grain elevator and flour mill in the 1870s. This was before settlers from Russia brought a new hard red winter wheat to Kansas and Nebraska. This wheat, called Turkey Red, survived hot summers and made possible the growing of wheat in the plains states. With all the wheat coming from the plains, Kansas City grew into a great milling and baking center. By the beginning of the twentieth century, Kansas City had almost thirty grain elevators. Thousands of people worked in the city's cracker companies and bakeries. Sunshine Biscuits started in Kansas City and developed into a national company, selling cookies, crackers, and candy.

Kansas City's first cattle show was held in 1899 when the American Hereford Association organized the National Hereford Show in a tent at the Kansas City Stockyards. In 1900, the show featured Hereford and Shorthorn cattle. The cattle show was named the American Royal in 1901. By 1902, the show had grown to include other livestock, and in 1905 riding and driving horses became part of the annual show. In the 1920s, many different activities became part of the American Royal, such as livestock judging and meetings for agriculture students. One of these meetings led to the founding of the Future Farmers of America (FFA) in 1928. The FFA still holds its annual meeting in Kansas City during the American Royal.

Until the twentieth century, when its economy became more diverse, Kansas City was known as the town built on "beef and bread." While Kansas City is no longer a "cowtown," it is still a leading grain center. Farmers ship corn and wheat to Kansas City, where it is stored in huge grain elevators for later shipment to milling companies.

Cattle in holding pens at the Kansas City stockyards. (Missouri State Archives)

Kansas City's stockyards were built in the 1870s. They covered about fifteen acres near the junction of the Missouri and Kansas rivers. The stockyards were a maze of wooden holding pens and pathways. Each day animals were herded along a wooden path to one of the meatpacking plants. By the turn of the century, Kansas City was the country's second largest meatpacking center.

Four national meat companies and several smaller firms had plants in Kansas City. In peak years, about ten thousand workers labored in the plants. The meat companies sent agents to European countries to recruit workers for the packinghouses. Many of the workers came from Slavic countries. Men and women worked ten- and twelve-hour days in the "pig mills." Their jobs were difficult, and working conditions were grim. Before workers formed unions, a typical wage was twenty cents an hour. Jobs depended on the market prices of livestock. When prices were high, less meat was sold, and jobs were cut until demand for meat increased.

Many changes in the meat trade took place after World War II. A big flood in 1951 damaged Kansas City's packinghouses, causing a decline in production. Most of the companies were gone by the mid-1970s. The stockyards closed in 1991.

Today the cattle market is controlled by several large national companies. These companies often buy their cattle directly from feedlots or sale barns instead of at stockyards.

The Stove and the Icebox

See that the wood-box is full at night, and the shavings and kindlings in their place. In the morning empty the ash-pan, or better still, clean your stove or range at night.

—From *Practical Housekeeping*, 1880s

In colonial America, settlers cooked over fire. Two hundred years later, not much had changed. Women still cooked in fireplaces, in both the city and the country. Houses often had summer kitchens with brick ovens away from the main kitchen. Cooking over fire required simple preparation methods. When the cast-iron range, or cookstove, was introduced, women had to learn new ways of cooking.

The first "range" was developed in the late 1700s by Benjamin Thompson, an Englishman. When his diagrams and explanations became available in the United States, foundries began making ranges in large numbers. The cities of Albany and Troy, in New York, were centers for range manufacturing in the 1800s.

The new ranges were large and required lots of wood. Later models had many doors for ovens and fireboxes. Ranges were

BAKING JOHNNY CAKE.

A woman baking johnnycakes. The cornmeal batter was put on a slab and placed at an angle for baking on the hearth. (State Historical Society of Missouri)

not an immediate success. They did not reduce women's work. The fire had to be kept burning, the ashes emptied, the oven cleaned, the wood stored. It wasn't until the 1870s that ranges became easier to use.

Using the new ranges required patience and skill. A nineteenth-century cooking guide gave this advice on baking a cake: "If the hand can be held in from 20 to 35 seconds, it is a 'quick oven,' and from 35 to 45 seconds is 'moderate,' and from 45 to 60 seconds is 'slow.'"

Around 1900, ranges were redesigned to burn coal. Wood had become too expensive to transport to the growing cities. Coal was easier to ship and took up less storage space at home. A big problem with coal was having ashes and black soot in the kitchen. But there was no going back. The Machine Age had come to the kitchen.

An iron range with a water reservoir on the right. (State Historical Society of Missouri)

Gas ranges with burners and ovens soon replaced coal-burning ranges. For the first time, cooks were able to regulate cooking temperatures. They simply raised or lowered the gas flame. Kitchens became cleaner, and cooking became easier. Even the look of the gas range reflected the new age—sleek, white, and modern. Next came the electric range. These improvements freed women from tending the oven. In time, with automatic controls, women could safely leave home with dinner in the oven.

People in rural areas were slower to acquire gas and electric ranges. They had ample supplies of wood, and some saw

In the 1930s, magazines featured advertisements promoting "modern" electric ranges. (Kansas City Power & Light Co.)

no need for the newfangled ranges. Most country homes had no electricity until the 1930s when the Rural Electrification Administration (REA) brought power lines to rural areas. After World War II, most country people joined the kitchen revolution and put their wood cookstoves to rest.

Laura Ingalls Wilder, the famous Missouri author of the Little House books, was one country dweller who had a modern kitchen in the early 1900s. She was quite proud of her 1908 cookstove from Montgomery Ward, the hot and cold running water, and the low wood cabinets her husband designed for her height (she was five feet tall). The Wilders' kitchen once won an award as the "most modern Ozark country kitchen."

Keeping Foods Cold

At the time of the Revolutionary War, Thomas Jefferson was storing ice and making ice cream at Monticello. In rural

Columbia Ice & Cold Storage, 1900. (State Historical Society of Missouri)

areas, people chopped ice from streams and ponds and stored it in belowground icehouses. For city dwellers, a privately owned icehouse was not always practical or possible. Instead, they made daily trips to the market to buy fresh foods.

An icebox was patented in 1803 by Thomas Moore, a Maryland farmer. It was a wooden chest with an upper compartment to hold ice and a lower compartment for food. The cooled air moved down to the lower compartment and cooled the food. A drip pan underneath caught melted water.

In the 1830s, Nathaniel Wyeth of Cambridge, Massachusetts, invented a machine to cut ice in blocks of one size. This machine, pulled by a horse over frozen ponds, cut grooves in the ice that made it look like a checkerboard. These large blocks were sawed and pulled from the pond. With this invention, ice became a business. Many homes and businesses soon had iceboxes that held blocks of machine-cut ice.

When iceboxes became common in the mid-nineteenth century, it was finally possible to keep food cool in warm seasons. In cities, the ice wagon and the iceman became a familiar sight. Every day, families hung signs in a window or on the porch telling the iceman how much ice they needed. Home delivery of ice—usually from May to October—was a thriving business all across the country.

In 1834, a patent for an ice-making machine was given to Jacob Perkins, a New Englander. Although a mechanical refrigerator was invented in the 1830s, it wasn't until the 1930s that refrigerators became a part of most American homes. By that time, electricity to power the new machines was widely available. The electric refrigerator eliminated the job of the iceman. It also eliminated an annoying job for family members—emptying the drip pan under the icebox.

The invention of the cold-storage room and the refrigerated railroad car enabled perishable foods to be shipped across the country. Farmers earned more money by shipping their fruits and vegetables long distances. They could hold their produce in storage, waiting for higher prices. Wholesale fruit and vegetable merchants stored large quantities of produce for later shipment. Meat companies made heavy use of refrigerated railroad cars.

There had been experiments with mechanical freezing systems for food in the late nineteenth century. After many years of research, an American engineer, Clarence Birdseye, developed a quick freezing method in the early 1920s. Birdseye is considered the founder of the frozen food industry. His company marketed the first "family-sized" packages of frozen food in 1925. Birdseye sold his company in 1929; it became the General Foods Corporation. He continued his research and later invented a method for dehydrating food. When he died in 1956, he was the owner of about three hundred patents.

Frozen foods were not accepted quickly by American consumers. Food companies spent much time and money developing better freezing machinery and advertising their new products. It wasn't until the 1940s that the frozen-food industry became profitable.

During World War II, meats were rationed, and frozen-food

lockers were established in many communities. Farm families froze their home-produced meats, vegetables, and fruits and made weekly trips to pick up their "groceries" from the locker.

The first TV dinner (turkey and gravy with corn bread, yams, and peas) came on the U.S. market in 1954. Invented by Swanson Foods, this new product became a great success. Even the boxes of the early Swanson dinners were designed to look like televisions. The original Swanson's TV dinner tray is in the collection of the Smithsonian Institution. Today American shoppers spend more than $3 billion a year on frozen dinners.

The Marketing of Food

Early markets developed when local farmers got together to sell their produce to people in towns and cities. Until the mid-1800s, most people tended home gardens, had milk cows, and raised pigs and chickens. Three things happened to change this pattern of food supply: the expansion of railroads, the growth of towns and cities, and the development of new ways of selling food.

Railroads improved the quantity and quality of food available in the United States. City dwellers could buy fresh dairy products and eggs. Refrigerated cars transported exotic fruits from the tropics. In small towns, general stores opened to serve the surrounding communities. Trains brought many supplies to these all-purpose stores. The general store sold basic foods in bulk. There were barrels and tins of rice, beans, crackers, sugar, and flour. Candy, fabric, clothing, tools, tea, and coffee arrived by rail.

New Ways to Market

In 1859, a store opened in New York City that paved the way for the modern supermarket. It was named the Great American Tea Company, and its owners were George Hunting-

A scene at Union Market in St. Louis, 1893. (State Historical Society of Missouri)

ton Hartford and George F. Gilman. The two men had big ambitions for their small store. They bought tea in large quantities, asking sellers for cheaper prices. They tried to buy directly from producers to avoid middlemen. Later they began their own importing business for coffee, spices, and other products. Hartford and Gilman passed the savings from their new buying practices to their customers. They offered lower prices than other merchants. They also enticed customers with contests and publicity gimmicks.

Hartford and Gilman were pioneers in another very important way. They weren't satisfied with just one store. So they opened a second store, then a third, and by 1912 they owned almost five hundred grocery stores across the country.

Beal's Grocery in Independence, early 1900s. (Missouri State Archives)

The store name was changed in 1869 to the Great Atlantic & Pacific Tea Company—A&P for short.

It seemed like the growth of A&P wouldn't stop. More and more stores opened. By 1930, there were more than fifteen thousand A&Ps. One unfortunate aspect of this growth was the decline of independent grocery stores. Many people remember the corner grocery store, or the "mom-and-pop" store. Customers could buy on credit and have food delivered to their homes. Corner stores could not buy in large quantities, nor could they offer much variety. Their demise was inevitable with the coming of the automobile. With the automobile, people began to shop away from their neighborhoods.

Missouri's excellent rail and river services attracted many food companies to the state. The advertisement above and the one on the right, both from 1904, promoted Missouri food businesses. (Syrup label from the Missouri State Archives)

Today's small "convenience" stores have many of the features of the old corner store—limited selection, higher prices, and credit (with credit cards). But they are usually chain stores, not locally owned.

Brand Names and Packaging

Along with chain stores came the introduction of brand-name products and packaging. One of the earliest packaged products was a cereal invented by a Michigan doctor named John H. Kellogg.

Kellogg worked for a sanatorium founded by Mother Ellen Harmon White, a religious leader. White had some strange ideas about food. For example, her patients with high blood

pressure were made to eat ten to fourteen pounds of grapes a day. Thin patients had to eat twenty-six meals a day and stay in bed with sandbags on their stomachs. White believed in large doses of bran, small portions of meat, and no salt, liquor, or tobacco. For White's patients, Kellogg created Granose, a granola-like cereal. He thought people should chew dry and brittle foods to keep their teeth healthy.

It so happened that Charles Post was a patient of Dr. Kellogg's. Both of these men established companies that became famous for dry cereals such as Post Grape Nuts and Kellogg's Corn Flakes. They spent millions of dollars advertising their cereals as foods for good health. This advertising convinced millions of Americans to change their breakfast habits and eat processed instead of cooked foods. Kellogg and Post were among the first businessmen to promote "health foods." Whether their claims were justified is open to debate. A recent health fad is oat grain cereals. "Puffed" oat cereal costs about thirty cents per ounce; cooked oatmeal costs about five cents per serving.

Packaging became possible when machines to make containers were invented. The first paper bag was made in Pennsylvania in 1852. Paper bags became common in stores after the Civil War. The foldable cardboard box was produced in New York in 1879. As rail service expanded, more food was transported in containers. Companies needed to identify their products, so they printed their names on boxes and cartons. Soon they added trademarks, then slogans and drawings.

Mass marketing truly arrived when products were sold in individual containers. The product became identified with the package. Think of the Morton Salt girl, the Quaker on Quaker Oats, the arm and hammer on the baking-soda box, or P. T. Barnum's animals on the animal-cracker box. Advertising encouraged consumers to believe in brand names. Companies promised purity, high quality, convenience, and low cost from brand-name products. These promises led to the use of additives in canned and processed foods. Additives improved the appearance of foods and provided longer life on grocery store shelves. The cheapest additive is air. One ounce of grain (two tablespoons), puffed with air, becomes a large bowl of cereal at a high price.

Changes on the Farm

In the early 1800s, most Missouri farms were small. Later some farmers operated large farms where they grew cotton and tobacco. These large farms needed the labor of many people, and their owners usually had slaves. After the Civil War, the number of farms increased in Missouri. By the 1890s, there were more than two hundred thousand farms in the state.

Agriculture was changing all across the country between 1860 and 1900. In the 1860s, 80 percent of Americans lived on farms. More than 400 million acres of virgin soil became farmland. These decades of expansion brought change to all ways of life in the United States.

In Missouri, farmers began producing more hogs and cattle and raising more horses and mules. They also grew more corn, hay, wheat, barley, oats, grapes, and apples. New farm machines helped the farmers in their work. Reapers, threshers, binders, balers, corn planters, and plows with wheels made farms more productive. In 1840, it took 233 hours to produce a hundred bushels of wheat. By 1920, it only took 87 hours for the same job.

The Missouri State Board of Agriculture was created in 1865. It provided information and training on new farm ma-

A threshing crew near Corder, 1893. (Missouri State Archives)

The Griffin-McCune Farmstead Historic District in Pike County. This unusual octagonal barn was used to store grain and house livestock. (Missouri Department of Natural Resources)

chinery and better ways of farming. The School of Agriculture at the University of Missouri accepted its first students in the fall of 1870. Scientists at the school experimented with seeds and soils and new ways to raise livestock and crops. This research continues today with the school's focus on food production for the twenty-first century.

Passenger Pigeons Darken the Sky

Americans have been great hunters from the time of the Indians to the present day. One bird that required little hunting skill was the passenger pigeon. In their explorations, Jacques Cartier and Samuel de Champlain wrote of millions of passenger pigeons that "darkened the sky." This was no exaggeration. There were so many passenger pigeons that a single flock could take several hours to pass across the sky. One man who studied birds told of a flock a mile wide and 240 miles long!

Peter Matthiessen, in his book *Wild Life in America*, said that passenger pigeons were "the most numerous bird ever to exist on earth." He estimated that there were 9 billion passenger pigeons in North America at one time. The pigeon was cheap food, easily taken, and eaten by many in Missouri and throughout the nation. But its huge numbers created trouble for farmers. The bird became a pest because it ate farm crops.

An orgy of hunting eliminated the passenger pigeon by the twentieth century. The last passenger pigeon was killed in 1900.

The Second Wave of Immigrants

He who crosses the ocean, buys his own house.

—Italian saying

At the end of the nineteenth and the beginning of the twentieth century, millions of new immigrants came to the United States from Europe. They came to find a better life.

In 1907, more than a million people made the long journey from Europe to the United States. This year is considered the peak year of immigration. Most of the immigrants came from eastern and southern Europe. They settled in all parts of the country, especially in large cities where factories needed cheap labor.

Missouri was one of the states that attracted these new immigrants. As we have seen, a large number of Germans came to Missouri beginning in the 1830s. According to the 1850 census, the foreign-born population of St. Louis was 60 percent, the highest percentage in the United States. By 1890, St. Louis had 66,000 German-born people. It also had a large Irish population. By 1930, the city had settlements of people

A statue dedicated to Italian
immigrants in St. Louis.
(A. E. Schroeder)

from Italy, Russia, Poland, Greece, Romania, Hungary, Czecho-
slovakia, Croatia, and Serbia. Across the state, Kansas City's
grain and cattle businesses and its importance as a railroad
center brought thousands of European immigrants to town.
In 1920, Kansas City had 27,320 foreign-born people.

Wherever they settled, immigrants felt more comfortable
living with others from their own countries. Their communities were given names such as Little Italy, Kerry Patch, Bo-
hemian Hill, and Greektown. Missouri's total immigrant pop-

ulation never approached that of states like Illinois, Ohio, and New York. But it was big enough to add color and diversity to the state.

An item in the *St. Louis Post-Dispatch* in the early 1900s took note of this diversity: "If all the different kinds of people in St. Louis wore in the streets of the city all the different kinds of costumes they wore in their native countries before they came here, we might put a fence around the city and charge an admission fee."

Hoping for a Good Year

Many food traditions have grown around hopes for good fortune in the new year. Some of these traditions are still observed in Missouri.

German families place cherry branches in water on St. Barbara's Day, December 4. If the buds on the branches bloom on Christmas Eve, the new year will be good. Slavic people plant wheat seeds in a dish on St. Lucy's Day, December 13. If the wheat grows, a good year will follow. Italians eat lentils on New Year's Eve in hopes for a prosperous new year. African Americans eat black-eyed peas in dishes like "Hoppin' John" for good luck in the new year. Czechs eat the ear of a pig or hog jowl to ward off bad luck in the new year. Jews eat an apple slice dipped in honey, which promises a sweet year to come.

An Ethnic Sampler

Italians

A small number of Italians lived in Missouri before statehood. But not until the 1880s did Italians come to Missouri in large numbers. They came from northern and southern Italy and from Sicily. Some settled in the Ozarks area near St. James, and others found work in the mines of north Missouri. Most Italian immigrants settled in the cities.

St. Louis has one of the oldest Italian communities in the United States. Many of the early St. Louis Italians came from northern Italy, where they had been farmers, growing crops and producing wine. The land they worked was owned by wealthy families who refused to sell parcels of their land to the farmers. The Italians who came to St. Louis worked in clay pits, brickyards, and other factories where unskilled labor was needed.

Most of Kansas City's Italians came from southern Italy and Sicily. In Kansas City, Italians were employed as railroad, factory, and packinghouse workers.

The Italians were like others who came to the United States in hopes of escaping poverty and finding new opportunities. A typical pattern with "second-wave" immigrants was for the men to come first, later sending for wives and other family members. Once they saved some money, many Italians opened saloons, which became gathering places for the neighborhood. They also opened small family-run grocery stores. These stores sold the foods that were needed for Italian cooking, such as garlic, olive oil, pasta, cured meats, and cheese. In both St. Louis and Kansas City, southern Italians and Sicilians became fruit and vegetable dealers.

The neighborhood bakery was another important business in Italian communities. Italians wanted good bread with their meals as well as special breads and pastries for celebrations and feast days. Every day they purchased fresh bread from the bakeries. In the area called The Hill in St. Louis, many older people remember horse-drawn bread wagons coming through the neighborhoods. The bakeries made cookies with ingredients such an anise, sesame seeds, and almond paste. These breads and cookies are available today in Italian bakeries in St. Louis and Kansas City.

Pizza is an Italian food famous throughout the world. The origin of pizza is uncertain, dating back hundreds of years. It was then a simple flat bread covered with herbs, oil, and cheese. Pizza is often associated with Naples, Italy. It was a common food in that southern Italian city in the 1700s. When Italians added New World tomatoes to their pizza in the 1800s, its success was assured. In Missouri, St. Louis is known for its excellent pizza.

In 1910, St. Louis billed itself as the spaghetti center of the United States. At one time, the city had ten pasta factories. These factories, owned by Italian immigrants, were among the largest pasta producers in the country. The pasta business was well suited to a city located near major wheat-growing areas. The factories made pasta in hundreds of shapes from semolina wheat. One factory, the Ravarino and Freschi Macaroni Company, won international prizes for its La Terminese brand of pasta. There are no longer any Italian-owned pasta factories in St. Louis. The R&F company is still in business,

The Ravarino and Freschi Macaroni Company in St. Louis, 1920s.

but it was recently sold to a national company. It is the largest pasta factory in North America.

There were also pasta factories in Kansas City. One of the largest in the Midwest was the American Beauty Macaroni Company. It is now owned by a national company.

City people came to appreciate Italian food when they dined at restaurants operated by Italian immigrants. By 1920, St. Louis and Kansas City had many Italian restaurants and cafés. Today, as St. Louis residents know, a trip to The Hill means good food.

Eastern Europeans

Settlements of eastern Europeans are found across the United States—from the Bohemians on the Nebraska plains and the Dalmatians on the Pacific Coast to the Poles in Chicago and the Russian Jews in New York City.

The eastern Europeans who immigrated to Missouri found work mostly in the cities. The Soulard area in St. Louis was home to many of these immigrants. There they found work in

Charles Bratkowski of St. Louis with his homemade Polish sausage. (Joann Bratkowski Nichols)

breweries, mills, and factories. In Kansas City, they found work in packinghouses and factories. Their churches, clubs, and fraternal organizations became centers for social activities.

Many eastern European food traditions revolve around family events, music, and religious holidays. First communions, weddings, and funerals were occasions in which food played an important role. Food helped the immigrants to remember their old ways while adjusting to their new lives.

Whether it's called kielbasa, kobasica, or just plain Polish sausage, the sausage is a beloved food of eastern Europeans. What we know as the "Polish" sausage is made by many nationalities, but each recipe is different. All contain garlic, spices, fat, and a variety of meats packed into a casing or skin. Blood sausage is another popular specialty. Old-timers in Kansas City tell stories about their trips to the packinghouses to buy buckets of blood for their sausages. These sausages are made with meat, rice, spices, and blood. After baking, they become crisp and black.

Missouri's two largest cities are home to small populations of Greeks and other people from eastern Mediterranean areas such as Lebanon and Syria. In the early 1900s, the Greeks, especially in St. Louis, were known for their many restaurants, coffeehouses, and candy shops. Their mouthwatering pastries, like baklava, contain lots of honey and nuts.

Mexicans

Mexicans have lived and worked in Missouri since the days of the Santa Fe Trail. They came to the state in large numbers around the beginning of the twentieth century. Kansas City has the state's largest population of Mexicans. Companies recruited Mexicans to work on the railroads and in meatpacking plants. Mexicans were often not interested in becoming "Americanized" because many hoped to return to their country after working for a while in the United States. Most earned the low wages of unskilled workers; few actually returned to Mexico. Conditions improved after World War II, and new Mexican immigrants joined their relatives in Missouri. In addition to Kansas City, Mexicans live in St. Louis and in northwest, central, and southeast Missouri.

With its bold and earthy flavors, Mexican cooking is a blend of many cultures—Native American, Spanish, Portuguese, French, and African. Its most important ingredients are corn, beans, peppers, tomatoes, fish, beef, pork, rice, and cheese. More than a hundred types of chilis grow in Mexico, each with a different taste and degree of "heat." Both fresh and dried chilis are used in main dishes and in salsas, or sauces.

Corn is a mainstay in Mexican cooking, used to make tortillas, tamales, and breads. Herbs and spices such as coriander, oregano, and cinnamon provide spicy accents to simple foods. Each region of Mexico has its own dishes and ways of cooking.

The familiar taco stand does not represent the variety of Mexican food. It is becoming easier to find restaurants that serve more than tacos and tamales. It is also easier to find more ingredients for Mexican food in local grocery stores. A few years ago, shoppers could buy only green bell peppers and a few hot peppers in grocery stores. Now a greater range of chilis is available—from chilis jalapeños to chilis poblanos.

Jews

America has always meant a place of freedom for Jewish people. The first Jewish settlers sailed from Brazil to New York in 1654. From the 1700s to the present time, Jews have immigrated to America from all over the world. They came to escape persecution and poor conditions in their countries.

Beginning in the 1820s, German Jews settled in the United States. From 1881 until World War I, large numbers of eastern European Jews arrived on our shores. Most settled in cities, working at many different jobs—from merchants and tailors to actors and writers. Missouri has Jewish populations in its major cities as well as in small towns.

The Jewish religion has laws about food and diet. Some foods are forbidden. *Kosher* is the term used for those that are permitted. Kosher foods require slaughtering or handling under the supervision of a rabbi. Wherever they lived, Jews adapted local foods to their religious laws. Some favorite Jewish foods are kosher hotdogs, bagels, blintzes (filled pancakes), matzo balls, kreplach (dumplings filled with meat), gefilte fish (a stuffing or spread), cholent (a stew), and braided challah bread, usually eaten on the Sabbath. The Jews also make special foods for religious occasions.

Easter is observed among eastern Europeans with many food rituals. Poles, Czechs, and Croats take baskets of food to their churches on the day before Easter. The baskets line the main aisle of the church, and the priest blesses each one. Inside the baskets are eggs, salt, bread, sausage, and sometimes a candle. The eggs represent the beginning of life.

Decorated Easter eggs are a tradition of people from the Ukraine, Poland, Lithuania, Hungary, and Slovakia. Women begin painting dozens of eggs weeks before Easter. They use dye and wax to create beautiful and complex patterns. The eggs are given to family and friends and used in church services.

The ancient feast of Passover is celebrated by Jews in March or April. Passover commemorates the deliverance of the Hebrews from slavery in Egypt six thousand years ago. Passover is also called the Feast of the Unleavened Bread to symbolize the Hebrews' quick flight from Egypt. Jews eat many unleavened (without yeast) foods at Passover. Another special Passover food is *charoses*, a mixture of nuts, apples, wine, and spices. This dish symbolizes the bricks the Hebrews used to build the pyramids. It is served with bitter herbs to remind them of the bitterness of slavery.

Croatian women preparing *povitica*, a sweet bread with a ground-nut filling. (Marijana Grisnik)

The Croatians came from the country that until recently was known as Yugoslavia. In 1991, Croatia declared its independence from Yugoslavia. In the early 1900s, many Croatians settled in midwestern cities such as Chicago, Pittsburgh, Cleveland, Omaha, St. Louis, and Kansas City. Like other immigrant groups, the Croatians brought their "old-country" food traditions to their new country. They served special foods on holidays and especially at weddings.

A Croatian wedding was an exciting celebration that sometimes lasted two days. Hundreds of people were invited to the wedding mass and the reception afterward. Families and friends began preparing food weeks before the wedding. The men made arrangements for the hall where the reception would take place. They also bought the wine and beer.

The women prepared the wedding food. They gathered at the home of the bride to bake delicious breads and sweets. No wedding was complete without *sarma*, a roll of sour cabbage filled with ground beef, pork, rice, and spices. Few wedding guests could resist desserts such as *povitica* and *puhance*. Povitica is a bread filled with ground walnuts or hazelnuts, cocoa, and orange peel. The bread is shaped in loaves or coiled like a snake. Puhance is a fried pastry. It is shaped in bows, figure eights, and twists. Women spent days making bushels of puhance for weddings.

Neighborhood bands played music at Croatian weddings. The musicians used accordions and a stringed instrument called the *tamburitza*. The bands played polkas, waltzes, and tunes for a circle dance known as the *kolo*. The dancing and eating went on for hours. Then it was time for a well-deserved rest for the bride's and groom's parents!

Croatians still practice many of these wedding traditions today.

A Sweet Story

Sugar has a mysterious history. Many food historians believe that sugar originated in India in the time before Christ. Caravans traveling from India to the Near East brought sugarcane for planting. Sugar was introduced to the western world by Arabs. It became an important trade item of the Venetian empire. Portugal also became a major exporter of sugar. In these early days and up to the nineteenth century, sugar was an expensive product.

Columbus brought the first sugarcane to the islands of the New World on his second voyage in 1493. The Portuguese, French, Spanish, and Dutch soon established large plantations to grow this new crop on their islands. These plantations required many workers. Even the smallest sugar plantation had a workforce of hundreds. At first, native "Indians" worked the sugarcane fields. Then blacks from Africa were imported to replace the natives. It was sugar that introduced black slavery to the New World.

Sugar played a large part in the economy of the New England colonies. Ships from the colonies sailed to the Caribbean islands with cargoes of salt cod for the slaves of the sugar plantations. The ships sailed back to the colonies with sugar and molasses. The sugar was usually exported to Europe to

A boy with a cane of sweet sorghum.
Along with honey, sorghum molasses
was used to sweeten foods until the late
1800s when white sugar became widely
available and cheap enough for most
Americans. (Missouri State Archives)

bring a greater profit. The cheaper molasses was used as a
sweetener by American colonists. Surplus molasses made possible the development of the rum industry. New ships were
built, and these ships sailed to Africa with rum and salt cod
to trade for slaves.

Until the middle of the nineteenth century, cane sugar
was too expensive for most Americans. Molasses, maple sugar,
and honey were the popular sweeteners. Cane sugar became
cheaper in the 1880s, when Congress lifted a tax on imported
sugar. Sugarcane was cultivated in the southern United States
(Louisiana, Alabama, Florida, Georgia, and Mississippi), but
it was on a small scale compared to that of the West Indies.
Today only a small amount of sugar is made in the United
States, in southern Louisiana.

Most immigrant groups had their special sweets. The sweets
were often made for weddings, feast days, and family celebra-

tions. Some of these foods became known to the general population. Others were enjoyed only within the ethnic group.

Many cookbooks have been written about the hundreds of German sweets. There is cheesecake (*Käsekuchen*), found on most restaurant menus and at delicatessens. *Lebkuchen* (Lepp cookies to Missouri Germans) are spicy Christmas cookies filled with fruits and nuts. German bakers often make fruit and vegetable-shaped sweets with marzipan, an almond and sugar paste. Jelly doughnuts are a pre-Lenten treat in German-speaking countries. In the United States, they are found in most bakeries.

The Italians and the French aren't far behind the Germans in their love of sweets. From the Italians, we have cannoli, a crisp pastry tube filled with sweet cream cheese and fruit; panforte, a dark fruitcake made for Christmas; and many kinds of cookies (*biscotti*) made with almonds, hazelnuts, and spices.

Italians prepare a variety of sweets for family and religious celebrations. One of these celebrations takes place on March 19, the feast of St. Joseph. Many Italians set a "St. Joseph's Table," laden with foods for the poor. Italian churches in St. Louis and Kansas City celebrate the feast of St. Joseph with lavish food displays.

The French are world famous for their pastries and breads. Some of these are crepes, which are folded, thin pancakes with a sweet or savory filling; éclairs, which are crusty tubes filled with sweet cream; macaroons, which are light-as-air meringue cookies; and croissants, which are flaky crescent-shaped rolls.

Greeks and Middle Eastern people favor pastries rich with honey and nuts. Slavic people use walnuts and poppy seeds in cookies and breads. Famous Jewish sweets include *hammantaschen*, which are three-cornered cookies filled with prune paste or poppy seeds, and *rugelach*, a dough crescent filled with raisins and nuts.

Many cultures make some type of fried cookie or fritter. They come in many shapes and sizes. Mexicans call their fried cookies *sopapillas*, Romanians call theirs *papanasi*, and Ital-

David and Joanie Gessert own Candymaking Corp. in Lathrop. The Gesserts sell supplies and ingredients to candymakers across the country. They also sell many kinds of candy by mail. (Jim Curley)

ians call theirs *zeppole*. These sweets probably developed when ovens were unavailable or impractical.

Both original settlers and "second-wave" immigrants made desserts from Missouri's native foods. From pies bursting with native apples and berries, to persimmon bread and black walnut ice cream and fudge, Missouri has contributed some delicious treats to the nation's dessert tray.

World's Fair Food

Meet me in St. Louis, Louis,
Meet me at the Fair,
Don't tell me the lights are shining,
Any place but there.
                    —Official song of the 1904
                    St. Louis World's Fair

One of the grandest events in Missouri's history was the Louisiana Purchase Exposition of 1904, known as the St. Louis World's Fair. The fair celebrated the one hundredth anniversary of the Louisiana Purchase. More than 20 million people from all over the world visited the fair during its seven-month run.

St. Louis began building for the fair in 1901. The fairgrounds spread over most of Forest Park. Hundreds of buildings were constructed for the exhibits. Visitors saw great works of art and the latest inventions. They tasted the foods of other countries. And they learned about new advances in science and education. All the states (except Delaware) and many foreign countries had exhibits at the fair. There were wild-animal shows, castles, gardens, fountains, a 264-foot-

An aerial view of the St. Louis World's Fair, 1904. This photo was taken from a balloon. (State Historical Society of Missouri)

high Ferris wheel, and a clock made from flowers with hands seventy-four feet long. In addition, three of America's most popular foods were introduced for the first time at the fair: the hotdog, the ice-cream cone, and iced tea.

The frankfurter sausage in a roll was first sold at the fair. But the frankfurter itself was nothing new. Some historians claim it was introduced at the Chicago World's Fair in 1893 as part of a German exhibit. Others say that Antoine Feuchtwanger, a German from St. Louis, sold frankfurters before the Chicago fair. The hotdog got its name when T. A. Dorgan, a cartoonist, made a cartoon of a frankfurter with a head, tail, and legs. The cartoon character looked like a dachshund, and the frankfurter became known as the "hotdog."

One of the food stands at the fair was operated by a Syrian named Ernest A. Hamwi. He sold a type of waffle called a *zalabia*. At the stand next door was an ice-cream maker. One day he ran out of dishes and asked Hamwi for a waffle to hold the ice cream. Hamwi rolled up a waffle, placed the ice cream on top, and the ice-cream cone was invented. However, years before the fair, an Italian named Italo Marchiony had invented a mold for an ice-cream cone. It was a small round "pastry cup with sloping sides." He received a patent for this invention in 1904, just before the World's Fair. But Marchiony never put his invention into production.

Iced tea was a genuine World's Fair creation. Like the ice-cream cone, iced tea happened by chance. A group of tea producers from India set up a special pavilion to promote their tea. Most Americans drank Chinese tea at that time. The Indians wanted Americans to taste their tea. They were serving hot tea on a hot summer day. Few people wanted their tea. So they poured the tea into glasses filled with ice, and the new drink was a big hit.

For centuries, people have eaten crushed and ground peanuts in sauces and pastes. African tribes used ground peanuts in stews as long ago as the fifteenth century. The Chinese and Peruvian Indians also made foods from ground peanuts. But it wasn't until 1890 that peanut "butter" was invented by Ambrose Straub, a St. Louis doctor. Straub wanted a healthy and easy-to-digest food for his elderly patients. So he experimented and made a spread from ground peanuts. In 1903, he patented a "mill for grinding peanuts for butter." It was introduced at the St. Louis World's Fair.

Peanut butter is the most popular sandwich spread in the United States. About half of the peanuts grown in this country are used for peanut butter.

Cooking by the Book

Cookbooks tell us a lot about how people live, what they eat, and how different styles of cooking travel from one part of the country to another.

The first truly American cookbook, written by Amelia Simmons of Hartford, Connecticut, was published in 1796. Simmons's book, *American Cookery*, contained the first printed recipe for pumpkin pie. The book included many ingredients found only in America, like corn and Jerusalem artichokes, as well as recipes for American foods such as slaw, johnnycake, and Boston baked beans.

In 1827, the first cookbook written by an African American was published. The book was called *House Servant's Directory*. Its author, Robert Roberts, was a free black man who had worked in France and England and for the governor of Massachusetts. His book not only included recipes but also gave directions for setting a fine table and serving food.

The number of cookbooks grew in the 1800s, in part because of easily available printing and cheap paper. In the late 1800s and early 1900s, cookbooks taught housekeepers about nutrition and the foods of other countries. The famous *Fannie Farmer* cookbook was published in 1896. It was the first cookbook to use "correct measurements" instead of directions such

as "take a pinch of salt." Farmer's book listed ingredients first, and then directions. This has become the standard way of writing recipes in the United States.

One of the most popular modern cookbooks in the United States was written by a Missouri woman—Irma S. Rombauer of St. Louis. Her *Joy of Cooking* is considered a classic. It has sold more than 15 million copies and is still in print today.

Born in 1877, Rombauer traveled widely in her youth and spoke French and German. After her marriage, Rombauer became well known in St. Louis for her excellent meals. Her two children asked her to write a book of her favorite recipes. She finished the book in 1931 and published it herself. Later she rewrote the book, adding more recipes. This time a major company published the book. By 1953, the book had sold well over a million copies.

Rombauer's recipes are clear and easy to follow. She believed that cooking should be an enjoyable activity, and she often used humor in her instructions. With its thousands of recipes, her book is a kitchen encyclopedia.

Rombauer died in 1962 in St. Louis. She left a dependable guide to good cooking, beloved by millions of Americans.

Toward the Modern Age

At the time of the 1904 World's Fair, St. Louis had several thousand manufacturing companies. These companies produced all types of goods—from tobacco, stoves, and crackers, to firebrick, paper bags, and boots. St. Louis was ranked as the fourth largest manufacturing city in the United States. Its railroad station was the largest in the world, covering eleven acres. More than two hundred and fifty passenger trains arrived and departed from the station every day.

Food for the War Effort

World War I, which began in Europe in 1914, had a great impact on Missouri. Although the United States did not enter the war until 1917, farmers were asked to grow more grain and raise more livestock. This extra food helped feed the Allied armies in Europe. Missourians joined the rest of the country in eating less meat and planting vegetable gardens so more food could be shipped to Europe. They signed pledges promising to conserve food. Missouri was second in the country in the number of pledges signed by its residents. Missouri factories grew larger and increased production to supply clothing, ammunition, lead, and lumber for the war.

Posters and other advertisements urged Americans to conserve food during World War I and World War II. (Western Historical Manuscript Collection, University of Missouri–Columbia)

Social Change in the 1920s

When the war ended in 1918, the United States began a period of growth and change. Perhaps the most important social change was in the role of women. Gaining the vote in 1920 was the first step toward equal rights for women.

Women's lives were changing in other ways. More women began working outside the home in factories and offices, and more women entered college. Electricity, running water, and new kitchen appliances made food preparation easier, and more food was available in stores. The days of endless hours devoted to growing and preserving food were coming to a close.

The 1920s were good times for most Americans except farmers. With improved farming methods, farmers produced more food than was needed at home and abroad. They received lower prices for their crops. Many could not hold onto their land. The 1920 census showed that, for the first time in Missouri's history, more people lived in towns and cities than in rural areas.

Economic Decline

On October 29, 1929, the stock market crashed. The economy went into a decline that lasted through the 1930s. The Great Depression was the worst economic disaster in America's history. Banks closed, businesses shut down, and millions of people lost their jobs.

Almost half of Missouri's industrial workers lost their jobs during the Depression. In the cities, jobless and homeless people went to soup kitchens and stood in line for food. Many also went to live with farm relatives who were more self-sufficient and produced their own food. Agriculture suffered as record-breaking heat and drought damaged farm crops. Most people could afford only the basics. The Depression was especially hard on black Missourians. In the 1930s, many blacks organized to protest the lack of job opportunities.

Government programs created jobs for millions of people during the Depression. Social Security and the Rural Electrification Administration (REA) were two important government programs that came out of the Depression. The REA brought electricity to rural areas across the country. Before the REA, only 10 percent of Missouri farm families had electricity.

Until the 1930s, few Missourians thought about the future of wildlife. They assumed that wildlife would always be abundant. But in less than a century, hunters had destroyed most of the state's game and furbearing animals. Some species were nearly extinct. Wildlife habitat was destroyed by careless use of the land, the expansion of farming, and a growing population. Except for a few laws, Missouri's wildlife population was not "managed."

The Missouri Department of Conservation was formed through citizen action during the Great Depression. Groups of concerned Missourians joined forces to educate their fellow citizens about the loss of wildlife. The result of their efforts was a historic event in Missouri history—the passage of a constitutional amendment in 1936. At that time, voters approved the creation of the Conservation Commission. In 1937, the commission was formally established by the state. The commission hired scientists to study the state's wildlife, land, and water resources. Scientists reintroduced certain animals into the state. The commission also developed regulations to protect animals and their habitats. Hunting was strictly regulated until animal populations increased.

Missouri's Department of Conservation was the first such agency in the country. It remains a model of effective wildlife management and research. And Missourians continue to support the department by approving new taxes for the preservation of wildlife.

From Victory Gardens to Fast Food

World War II was a milestone in the country's history. The war ended the Depression and jump-started the engines of industry. The country was at war for four years. Thousands of Missouri men and women joined the military or served in other wartime jobs.

On the home front, Missourians planted "victory gardens" to show their support for the war. Farmers increased production for the war. All citizens used ration coupons to buy gas, tires, coffee, sugar, meat, and even nylon stockings. Advertisements in newspapers, on the radio, and in moviehouses encouraged Americans to conserve food. Posters everywhere urged Americans to do their part to help win the war. Women took jobs in factories where they made airplanes and other products for the war. Times were difficult, but the country united behind the war effort.

After the war, the country enjoyed a building and spending boom. Millions of houses were built, and people began moving from cities to the new suburbs. The automobile became common and necessary for travel from the suburbs to jobs in the city. Most homes had modern kitchen appliances. Supermarkets replaced neighborhood grocery stores, local mar-

An A&P store in St. Louis in the late 1940s. (State Historical Society of Missouri)

kets became scarce, and shopping centers opened away from Main Street or even outside town.

World War II also led to changes in American food products and eating habits. American servicemen and servicewomen had eaten many new foods overseas. They became more open to different tastes and ways of cooking. American magazines and book companies recognized this interest by publishing recipes for foreign dishes and cookbooks on foreign foods. New foreign restaurants began opening across the country.

In the 1950s, large food companies spent millions of dollars advertising their "convenience" foods. Their new products found a ready market. Frozen dinners, box meals, and snack foods answered a need for busy American families. Fast-food restaurants soon became part of the convenience trend. As more women entered the workforce, families began going out to eat in record numbers.

Many fast-food restaurants began as hamburger or ice-cream stands. The first McDonald's opened in 1955 with a limited menu. Today fast-food restaurants offer more varied menus, and some serve breakfast, lunch, and dinner. Fast food is a major growth area of the food-service industry.

The microwave oven gained acceptance in the 1980s. It increased Americans' use of convenience foods. Food companies developed new products just for the microwave.

In agriculture, new and expensive machines replaced old ways of farming. Farms became fewer and larger. Many farmers grew only one or two crops and used chemicals to increase production. The traditional family farm, where many different crops were grown, became a relic of the past. Farmers now make up less than 2 percent of the U.S. population.

The United States has come a long way since the pioneers learned about Native American corn. Today we know more about food and nutrition. Most of us say we want healthy foods and a better diet. Yet a walk down a supermarket aisle shows row upon row of processed and packaged foods, ready to be popped into a microwave oven. We have more food than ever before, but we are doing less cooking.

Change in the Air

There are signs of change in our attitudes about food. Farmers' markets are opening in both large and small towns. More people plant gardens and garden without chemicals. Grocery stores stock fruits and vegetables from faraway lands. New restaurants serve long-forgotten regional foods, and fast-food restaurants offer healthier meals. Popular television shows feature famous American and foreign chefs. Food and eating seem to be never far from our minds.

Missouri—an Agricultural Leader

One of Missouri's more than one hundred thousand farms. (Missouri Department of Conservation)

Agriculture is big business in Missouri. It is the state's number-one industry and largest employer. Products grown in Missouri find their way across the country and around the world.

Missouri has over one hundred thousand farms. These farms, both large and small, produced more than $4 billion worth of market items in 1992. More than $1 billion worth of products went overseas as exports. Missouri's farmers export soybeans, rice, wheat, cotton, seeds, meat, poultry, and animal fats.

This logo, seen on many products in grocery stores, identifies foods grown or made in Missouri. (Missouri Department of Agriculture)

In 1985, the Missouri Department of Agriculture started the AgriMissouri Program. This program identifies foods produced or processed in Missouri. The AgriMissouri label appears on many foods in grocery stores across the state. Hundreds of food producers take part in the program. They believe that Missourians will buy Missouri products when given a choice.

Immigration Continues—
the Third Wave

We are again seeing large numbers of immigrants coming to the United States, mostly Asians and Hispanics. These immigrants introduce their styles of cooking to the general population. They open grocery stores and restaurants. And they bring even more variety to the American table.

Thousands of Asian people displaced by the Vietnam War came to the United States in the 1970s. But even before the Vietnam War ended, the United States attracted small groups of refugees from Hungary, Cuba, and other countries. Today economic and political problems in Latin America, Asia, and eastern Europe bring new immigrants to the United States. The new immigrant population has increased from 1.5 million in 1960–1964 to 5.6 million in 1985–1990. Missouri is now home to new immigrants from Mexico, Nicaragua, Vietnam, Cambodia, Laos, India, and the former Soviet Union.

In their desire for familiar foods, these immigrants start grocery stores to serve their communities. Asian grocery stores stock many varieties of rice, noodles, tea, spices, and unusual items such as quail eggs and shark fins. Hispanic grocery stores offer chilis, beans of many colors and sizes, edible cactus,

Stores serving Asian people carry many kinds of rice in fifty-pound bags. (Margot Ford McMillen)

masa harina (corn flour), *chorizos* (sausage), and Mexican beer. These stores offer all kinds of products for those open to different taste experiences. New immigrants also open restaurants and hold festivals and street fairs that feature their traditional foods.

Like the immigrants who came before them, "third-wave" immigrants pass on the character of their culture through the sharing of food. New people, new ideas, new foods . . . it is a hopeful time for the future of American food.

For More Reading

Can You Trust a Tomato in January? by Vince Staten (New York: Simon & Schuster, 1993), covers "everything you wanted to know (and a few things you didn't) about food in the grocery store." This book is full of interesting food history and trivia.

Eating in America: A History, by Waverley Root and Richard de Rochemont (New York: William Morrow & Co., 1976), is one of the most informative books on American food.

Food in History, by Reay Tannahill (New York: Crown Publishers, 1988), is a classic work on the place of food in world history.

Hunter's Stew and Hangtown Fry: What Pioneer America Ate and Why, by Lila Perl (New York: Clarion Books, 1977), offers a look at food and food traditions in eighteenth- and nineteenth-century America.

Red-Flannel Hash and Shoo-Fly Pie: American Regional Foods and Festivals, by Lila Perl (Cleveland: The World Publishing Co., 1965), presents the food history of all regions of the country.

Slumps, Grunts, and Snickerdoodles: What Colonial America Ate and Why, by Lila Perl (New York: Clarion Books, 1975), describes the foods of Native Americans and New England, Middle Atlantic, and Southern colonists.

Why We Eat What We Eat: How the Encounter between the New World and the Old Changed the Way Everyone on the Planet Eats, by Raymond Sokolov (New York, Summit Books, 1991), begins with Columbus and ends with the new American cuisine.

Your library can help you find these books and other materials on food and cooking.

Index

Price, General Sterling, 64
Prohibition. *See* Volstead Act
Puhance, 114
Pumpernickel bread, 21, 48

Quaker Oats, 96

Raccoons, 36
Railroads, 39, 52, 63, 70, 76–
    78, 80, 91, 103, 106, 110, 125
Randolph, Vance, 24
Ravarino and Freschi Macaroni
    Company, 106–7
Reconstruction, 70
Red-eye gravy, 31
Refrigeration, 59, 88–90. *See
    also* Preservation
Renault, Philippe François, 66
Restaurants, 70, 72–73, 107,
    109, 131–32, 135
Revolutionary War, 87
River Des Peres, 10
Roberts, Robert, 123
Romania, 103
Romanians, 117
Rombauer, Irma S., 124
Rosati, Bishop Joseph, 54
Rosati, Missouri, 54
Rural Electrification Adminis-
    tration (REA), 87, 127
Russia, 47, 80, 103
Rye bread, 21, 48

St. Barbara's Day, 111
Ste. Genevieve, Missouri, 11
St. James, Missouri, 54, 105
St. Joseph, Missouri, 56, 75, 79
St. Joseph's Table, 117
St. Louis: founding of, 14;

trade and transport center,
    14–15, 74–75, 125; Soulard
    Market, 16–17; brewing in-
    dustry, 55–57; African Amer-
    ican migration to, 69–70;
    immigration to, 102, 104–7,
    109, 113; in the 1800s, 18;
    food companies, 106
St. Louis World's Fair, 119–22
St. Lucy's Day, 105
St. Martin's Day, 49
St. Nicholas Day, 49
St. Vrain, Jacques, 55
Saline County, Missouri, 3, 41
Salsas, 109
Salt, 4, 10, 22–23, 29, 31, 63,
    96
Samp, 8
Santa Fe Trail, 79
Sarma, 114
Sassafras, 12
Sauerkraut, 47
Sauk Indians, 5
Sausage, 48, 108–9, 112
School of Agriculture (Univer-
    sity of Missouri), 100
Scotland, 35
Sedalia, Missouri, 42–44, 56
Serbia, 103
Shawnee Indians, 5
Shrove Tuesday, 12
Sicily, 105
Simmons, Amelia, 123
Slovakia, 112
Snack foods, 132
Social Security, 127
Soulard, Antoine, 16
Soulard, Julia, 16
Soulard Market, 16–17